ALSO BY MATTHEW SPIELER

Selecting a President (with Eleanor Clift)

FUNDAMENTALS OF AMERICAN GOVERNMENT

★ ★ ★   ★ ★ ★

THE U.S. HOUSE OF REPRESENTATIVES

MATTHEW SPIELER

THOMAS DUNNE BOOKS
ST. MARTIN'S PRESS
NEW YORK

THOMAS DUNNE BOOKS.
An imprint of St. Martin's Press.

THE U.S. HOUSE OF REPRESENTATIVES. Copyright © 2015 by Matthew
Spieler. All rights reserved. Printed in the United States of America. For
information, address St. Martin's Press, 175 Fifth Avenue, New York,
N.Y. 10010.

www.thomasdunnebooks.com
www.stmartins.com

Designed by Steven Seighman

Library of Congress Cataloging-in-Publication Data

Spieler, Matthew, author.
   The U.S. House of Representatives : the fundamentals of American
government / Matthew Spieler.
       p. cm.
   Includes bibliographical references and index.
   ISBN 978-1-250-04036-7 (hardcover)
   ISBN 978-1-4668-3564-1 (e-book)
   1. United States. Congress. House.   I. Title.   II. Title: United
States House of Representatives.
   JK1319.S65 2015
   328.73'072—dc23
                                                      2015028828

Our books may be purchased in bulk for promotional, educational, or
business use. Please contact your local bookseller or the Macmillan
Corporate and Premium Sales Department at (800) 221-7945, extension
5442, or by e-mail at MacmillanSpecialMarkets@macmillan.com.

First Edition: December 2015

10 9 8 7 6 5 4 3 2 1

For Shannon

☆ CONTENTS ☆

★ ACKNOWLEDGMENTS ★

I am grateful to my former colleagues at Congressional Quarterly, who, during my brief tenure there, educated and mentored me. Thank you for teaching me how to bring politics to life in narrative form.

THE U.S.
HOUSE OF
REPRESENTATIVES

☆ INTRODUCTION ☆

On January 3, 2013, the House of Representatives convened in a new political landscape. Speaker John Boehner, an Ohio Republican, would be reelected to his leadership post, but with diminished support. Two years earlier, when the Republicans had regained control of the House, Boehner had been the unanimous choice of his Republican colleagues for Speaker. This time, twelve members of his own party had pointedly defected, choosing instead to either cast symbolic votes for others or for no one at all. Frustration with Mr. Boehner, a fixture in Washington since his election to a staunchly Republican district in 1990, had been growing among disgruntled conservatives for two years. The Republican Speaker, they argued, had been too lenient in his dealings with President Barack Obama, a Democrat who had just been reelected to a second term. One newly elected Republican member grumbled that his party's leader had "signed our country onto a fiscal suicide pact"[1] in his budget negotiations with the president.

Yet Boehner endured, winning another two years in the Speaker's chair with the votes of 220 of his colleagues.* His Democratic counterpart, Minority Leader Nancy Pelosi (D-CA), had received 192 votes for Speaker.[2] For Pelosi, the last six years had been exceptionally tumultuous. In 2006, she had led her party to victory in the midterm elections, returning the House to Democratic control for the first time in twelve years. Perhaps more importantly, she had been the first woman in American history elected Speaker of the House. Just four years later, having ushered much of President Obama's legislative agenda through Congress—including a landmark universal health-care bill, a major economic stimulus measure, and sweeping legislation overhauling the nation's financial regulatory laws—Pelosi found herself back in the role of Minority Leader. In fact, following the Democrats' epic losses in the 2010 midterm elections, some Democrats pushed for her departure from the Democratic

---

* On September 25, 2015, Boehner announced he was resigning his Speakership and his seat in the House.

2

leadership. Yet Pelosi, known for her political grit, survived and remained in her role as House Democratic Leader.

Indeed, the makeup of the House of Representatives—far more than the U.S. Senate—reflects the shifts in attitudes of the American public. When House Republicans gained 63 seats in 2010, enough to hand them a governing majority, Senate Democrats maintained a 6-seat majority in the Senate—where only (approximately) one-third of members stand for reelection every two years. In the House, where every representative is up for reelection in every election cycle, a change in the political mood of the country can bring about a swift and dramatic change in leadership—one that often has severe consequences for American governance. Following the 2010 midterm elections, for example, the newly elected Republican House majority brought the Obama administration's policy agenda to a screeching halt.

While the previous Democratic House leadership had used the chamber to serve as the legislative engine for Obama's policy priorities, the newly elected Republican House rammed through bills to cut federal spending on social programs, keep in place tax cuts enacted under the Bush administration in 2001 and 2003, and—perhaps most importantly—to repeal his signature health-care law, known as the Patient Protection and Affordable Care Act (or, more commonly, the Affordable Care Act).[3] Boehner succeeded in enacting spending cuts that most Democrats opposed, although Republican efforts to repeal the Affordable Care Act stalled in the Democratic-controlled U.S. Senate. House Republicans' efforts to make permanent the Bush-era tax cuts were also unsuccessful,[4] as Senate Democrats and the president held their ground. Despite these disappointments, the Republican "wave" of 2010 (a "wave election" refers to one in which one party makes dramatic, sweeping electoral gains) did change the trajectory of American political debates, at least for a time. In 2009 and 2010, the legislative focus of American politics was on a federal overhaul of American health-care policy, increased federal regulation of financial markets, and increased federal spending intended to stimulate the American economy. To be sure, those measures faced fierce Republican opposition. In the end, however, Obama and his Democratic allies prevailed, and all three became law.

Following the Republican wave of 2010, however, the focus of U.S. legislative debates shifted considerably. With respect to federal spending, the question concerned the depth and breadth of budget cuts—which programs should be slashed, and by how much funding should their budgets be reduced? Rather than considering legislation to expand access to health care, the House now spent its days devising legislative strategies to undo the universal health-care law that had already been enacted. While the House had powered Obama's legislative machine during his first two years in office, its newly empowered Republican leadership emerged as the most daunting obstacle to enacting his policy agenda. Despite the president's reelection in 2012—as well as a Democratic gain of 8 seats in the House[5]—the GOP remained in control of the chamber. Moreover, with the Democrats still firmly in control of the U.S. Senate through 2014, the Republican-controlled House remained at the center of opposition to President Obama's policy priorities.

All of this is to demonstrate that the House of Representatives—its membership, leadership, rules, and procedures—matter greatly. The House has played a critical role in virtually every major policy battle in American history—as will be demonstrated in the coming chapters. Understanding the way the House functions is vital to understanding American politics, and it is the purpose of this book to provide a basic guide to its history, structure, core functions, and culture.

1: ELECTION TO THE U.S. HOUSE

A s an institution, the House of Representatives has broad discretion to make its own rules. One rule dictated by the U.S. Constitution, however, is that its members stand for election every two years. This feature of the House is in marked contrast to the U.S. Senate, where members stand for election every six years—roughly one-third of the Senate seats are up for reelection every two years. This discrepancy explains, in part, why the House is more sensitive to shifts in public opinion—since every House seat is up for grabs in every regularly scheduled federal election, all members must attempt to win their districts in the same national political environment. For example, in 2010—which, as demonstrated earlier, was a very good year for Republicans nationally—the GOP gained 63 seats in the House. With all 435 House seats in contention, Republicans managed to win 242—more than enough for a majority. In the Senate, however, only 37 out of 100 Senate seats were up for election in 2010. Thus 63 senators did not have to face the voters. Democratic senators who were vulnerable to defeat were shielded from an electorate that was inclined to vote them out of office. In the House, however, no such shield exists.

Additionally, every person who uses the title "Representative" or "Congressman" or "Congresswoman" has won an election to represent his or her district in the House. Drawing attention to this fact may seem like stating the obvious, but this feature distinguishes the House from the U.S. Senate, in which senators can be appointed to vacant seats on an interim basis by their state's governor. (Senate seats often become vacant when senators are elected to other offices or retire before their term has expired.) Governors, however, have no power to appoint members of the House. If a member leaves the House before his or her term has expired, that member's seat remains vacant until the next election.

The electoral process that culminates in winning a House seat begins with a primary election. As with presidential elections, primary races for House seats serve as intraparty contests. Thus, all Democratic candidates for a House seat who have gathered the requisite legitimate signatures to gain ballot access compete against each other. Republican candidates for that same House seat will compete in their own primary election. The question of who is eligible to vote in such primary elections depends on the relevant state's election laws. States that hold closed primary elections only allow registered members to vote each party's contest. Thus, only registered Democrats can cast ballots in the Democratic primary election while only Republicans can participate in the Republican primary election. Registered independents usually cannot vote in closed primaries. Some states, however, allow independent voters to vote in either primary (but not in both). In each district, the winner of the Democratic nomination faces off against the Republican nominee in the general election held on the Tuesday after the first Monday in November.

In order to launch a viable bid for the House, a candidate must raise sufficient funds to support his or her campaign. Indeed, the cost of running for Congress has skyrocketed in recent years. In 2012 candidates who won election to the House spent roughly twice as much as victorious candidates did in 1986. Ironically, the competitiveness of House elections has waned during that same period.[1] Successful House candidates in 2012 spent an average of $1.6 million on their campaigns. In the most competitive House elections, however, victorious candidates spent on average $2.3 million to gain election to the chamber.

Money raised by a candidate's campaign pays for television (and radio) advertising that makes the case for that candidate's election, and attacks his or her opponent(s). These funds also pay for a professional campaign staff, office space, and for the candidate's expenses (hotel rooms, transportation, etc.).

Because of the fundraising abilities and political savvy usually required to win election to the House, successful candidates have often held previous offices. They may have served in state legislatures, city councils, or even held a state-wide elected office (such as state treasurer or state attorney general). At times, however, candidates with no prior political experience, no connections to major campaign contributors, or deep pockets, do successfully run for the House. These candidates often run as "political outsiders" and manage to use their lack of a professional political background as an asset. They run against "business as usual" in Washington, D.C., and brand themselves an "everyman" who will truly represent average Americans in Congress. Such candidates can be particularly successful in elections held in political environments in which the public has grown disenchanted with those in power.

In 2006, for example, a year in which strong anti-Republican sentiment dominated the political climate, Tim Walz, a high school teacher and retired National

Guard command sergeant major who had served in Afghanistan, launched a long-shot bid as a Democrat for Congress with no prior political experience. His opponent was Gil Gutknecht, a veteran Republican who had represented Minnesota's 1st Congressional District since 1994. Gutknecht was popular with his constituents, having been reelected to his seat two years earlier by a 25-point margin.[2] Known for his mild-mannered temperament and wonky demeanor, he had not been considered by most analysts to be in danger of losing his seat. But the 2006 elections featured a toxic environment for Republicans—President George W. Bush had become deeply unpopular nationally, and in the eyes of voters the Republican Party in Congress had been tainted by scandal. A disgraced Republican lobbyist named Jack Abramoff—who later served time in prison stemming from charges of conspiracy, fraud, and tax evasion—was found to have ties to a number of influential Republican congressmen, one of whom went to prison for his role in the scandal. Gutknecht, however, had no ties to Abramoff or any other scandal. By all accounts, he was a personally honorable man, and was not high on the Democrats' list of top targets in the 2006 elections.

When a political party faces a poisoned political environment, however, voter contempt for that party can be wide reaching and endanger politicians who in any other year would have no trouble being reelected. Such was the case with Gutknecht. To make matters worse for the Republican incumbent, Tim Walz—an energetic upstart candidate who proved to be a highly talented campaigner—was able to capitalize on voters' dissatisfaction with the governing Republican majority. He was able to cast himself as an outsider and use his lack of political experience as an asset in an election in which membership in the party in power was tantamount to being "part of the problem" in the eyes of many voters.[3]

The phenomenon of the victorious political outsider was also present in the 2010 congressional elections. This time, however, it was the novice Republican challengers who upset their Democratic incumbent counterparts. Republican Scott Rigell, for example—a car dealer based in Virginia Beach with no political experience—was elected to represent Virginia's 2nd Congressional District.[4] John Runyan, a former professional NFL football player, ousted Democratic incumbent John Adler in New Jersey's 3rd Congressional District.[5]

But at times an outsider's political success can be short-lived. Because they are often elected in unusual political climates, they may struggle to make headway in a normal electoral environment. In 2010, for example, Republican Joe Walsh managed to ride a national Republican wave to victory in a highly competitive congressional district in the Chicago suburbs.[6] Walsh, a staunch conservative who was unconventional in his personal style and prone to making gaffes in front of reporters and cameras, had tried and failed to run for office in the past. He had run unsuccessfully for Congress in 1996 against longtime Representative Sidney Yates, a liberal Democrat who had held his congressional seat since the Truman administration. Walsh earned considerable attention in the local press for his unorthodox campaign tactics, which included drawing attention to Yates's advanced age (he was eighty-seven) by throwing him a "birthday party."[7] In the end, Walsh—like many political outsiders—was rejected by the voters, losing to Yates by a whopping 26-point margin.[8] 1996, however, was not a "wave" election year. But 2010 was such a year, and a pro-Republican wave swept into office candidates who would have been highly unlikely to win an election in a year in which the Democrats and Republicans were largely on equal political footing. Sometimes these "accidental" congressmen and congresswomen are swept out of office as quickly as they were swept in. Walsh, who sought to win in a new (but also politically competitive) congressional district in the next election following a process known as "redistricting"—went down to defeat in 2012.

Often, political novices who run for Congress lose their first election. Yet even a losing bid for Congress can prove valuable over the long term, because a candidate's elevated profile can bolster a future bid for public office. In fact, the challenger who defeated Joe Walsh in 2012—an Iraq War veteran named Tammy Duckworth—had herself run unsuccessfully for Congress as a Democrat and political neophyte in 2006.[9] In her first election, Duckworth had been an inexperienced campaigner who nevertheless attracted attention from national Democrats, due in large part to a powerful personal story. In 2004, Lt. Colonel Duckworth, a member of the Illinois National Guard, had been working on a Ph.D. in political science when she was deployed as a helicopter pilot to Iraq. There, a rocket-propelled grenade hit her helicopter. She lost both legs and her right arm was badly damaged.[10]

While her military experience was likely a major asset in her first campaign, she faced a far more politically experienced Republican opponent, then-State Senator Peter Roskam. Although Duckworth lost to Roskam in 2006, she developed a reputation as a promising political talent among national Democrats. In 2009 President Obama nominated her to be Assistant Secretary for Public and Intergovernmental Affairs in the U.S. Veterans Affairs Department, thereby further elevating her national profile.[11] In 2012 Duckworth seized an opportunity to run for Congress against Joe Walsh, and won by a 9-point margin.

Roskam's election in 2006, however, provides a

more traditional example of a politician's path to the House. After earning a law degree he worked as a legislative aide to two powerful Republican congressmen, Rep. Henry Hyde (R-IL) and Tom DeLay (R-TX), who eventually rose through the GOP leadership to be the #2 ranking Republican in the House. Roskam first ran for public office himself in 1992, winning a seat in the Illinois General Assembly. (Most state legislatures mirror the legislative branch of the federal government, and therefore have a state senate [the "upper" body] and a state house or state general assembly [the "lower" body].) Roskam went on to serve in the Illinois State Senate in 2000, a position he held until his election to the House. He had also run unsuccessfully for the House in 1998, having lost to fellow Republican Judy Biggert in the primary election. Thus, by the time he ran for the House in 2006, he was a seasoned political veteran, an experienced campaigner, and already had the fundraising apparatus required to wage a competitive race for Congress.[12] Moreover, Roskam's tenure in the Illinois state legislature had gained him fans and allies by the time he sought national office again in 2006. His antitax positions, for example, had earned him high praise from Americans for Tax Reform, the conservative advocacy group run by antitax crusader and powerful Republican operative Grover Norquist.[13]

While some House candidates win elections largely without the help of their national political party, this remains the exception to the rule. Most candidates want their party's national campaign organizations to aid their efforts and spend money on their behalf. In the House, each major political party has its own nationally based campaign apparatus. The Democratic Congressional Campaign Committee (DCCC) and the National Republican Congressional Committee (NRCC) support the campaign efforts of their candidates in districts throughout the country. Generally speaking, these organizations support the winners of their party's respective primary elections. In certain instances, a campaign committee will actually take sides in a primary—particularly when one candidate is seen as more likely than his or her primary opponents to win the general election.

Occasionally, a campaign committee intervenes in a primary only to see the voters thumb their noses at the establishment's preferred candidate. Such was the case in 2006 when the DCCC decided to intervene in the Democratic primary in New Hampshire's 1st Congressional District. With Democrats appearing poised for major gains that year—and given that NH-1 was (and remains) a highly competitive district—Democratic insiders sought to bolster the person whom they believed would be the strongest candidate against incumbent Republican Jeb Bradley. Thus, the DCCC threw its support to Rep. Jim Craig, the party's leader in the New Hampshire State House. Nationally based

Democratic campaign operatives viewed Craig as a far stronger candidate in the general election than fellow Democrat Carol Shea Porter, a social worker with no political experience. But at the grass-roots level, Shea Porter had strong support—particularly among liberals.

Despite the DCCC's intrusion into the race, Shea Porter won the Democratic primary overwhelmingly, defeating Craig 54 to 34 percent (with the remainder of the votes going to other Democratic candidates). Following Porter's upset victory in the primary, national Democrats still failed to take her candidacy seriously and took no action on behalf of their new nominee. Despite being left to fend for herself financially, Shea Porter won the general election, ousting the Republican incumbent and becoming the first woman ever elected to Congress from New Hampshire.[14]

While candidates do win without the support of their party's campaign committees, having such institutional support is generally viewed as desirable. In order to gain the attention and support of the DCCC or NRCC, a candidate must demonstrate that he or she is worthy of the party's investment. While the parties' campaign committees support their nominees in virtually all House races, they only devote financial resources to those whom they believe have a good chance to prevail in a competitive general election. Candidates seek to prove they are able campaigners by demonstrating they can raise money, connect with voters, attract positive attention in the press, and "stay on message"—a political mantra that refers to a candidate's ability to make a disciplined and persuasive case for his or her candidacy.

A candidate's fundraising prowess is important, not only to attract support from the party's campaign committee early on, but also to ensure that his or her message reaches the voters. This requires, among other things, considerable expenditures on television advertising. To fund a competitive race for Congress, a candidate can turn to a number of sources. The political parties' campaign committees spend money on their behalf and buy advertising in local media markets. Candidates themselves can also raise money from individuals inside or outside their districts. Outside groups (entities with a political agenda that are technically unaffiliated with the two political parties) can also spend heavily in House races.

These outside groups—commonly known as "527s" (a reference to their tax label) are technically prohibited under federal election law from coordinating their activities with candidates' campaigns. While a group may intervene in a race in which it shares a political philosophy or objective with one of the candidates, it is illegal for that group to carry on a collaborative relationship with that candidate or with their campaign. Moreover, the role of 527s in elections was transformed by two critical court decisions. The first decision, handed down by the U.S. Supreme Court, in *Citizens United v. Federal Election Commission* (2010),[15] held that the federal government could not set limits on independent political spending. In the second decision, *Speechnow.org v. Federal Election Commission* (also issued in 2010),[16] the D.C. Court of Appeals barred the federal government from limiting financial contributions by individuals to independent groups. These decisions paved the way for the rise of so-called "Super PACS," which flooded races in the last election cycle (2012) with corporate and union money.

My emphasis on candidates' fundraising and political advertising may have left the impression that campaigns are waged entirely through an advertising air war. A candidate who represents a House district that is home to roughly 500,000 residents cannot expect to personally meet all of his or her constituents, so a great deal of campaigning is done through television. But such advertising does not constitute the entirety of a campaign. Candidates also strive to meet voters in person, shaking hands on street corners and holding public events at restaurants, schools, local community centers, and so on. They give their "stump" speech—a candidate's standard pitch on the campaign trail. (This speech changes little if at all from day to day; it encapsulates a candidate's core message to the voters.)

After nearly two years of giving speeches, attending

local community events, and raising money, Election Night brings the campaign season to a close. As election returns trickle in from around the country, the makeup of the newly elected House begins to take shape, although some races may not be officially decided for days or even weeks after Election Day. While all House races are decided by the voters on Election Day, House elections can also occasionally take place outside of a regularly scheduled campaign season. A so-called special election takes place when a House seat becomes vacant. Thus, if a House member resigns from his or her seat in July, a special election may be held to replace that member in the months following the resignation. Voter turnout (which refers to the number of eligible voters who go to the polls to participate in an election) is typically far lower in special elections because they often feature only one contest, whereas during a regularly scheduled election voters may cast ballots for the House, U.S. Senate, state legislature, city council, and more.

A successful candidate for the House experiences a period of political limbo between his or her election and being sworn into office. A candidate who wins a House seat during a regularly scheduled November election will not officially become a congressman or congresswoman until early January. In the interim two-month period, he or she is addressed as "Representative-Elect" or "Congressman/

Congresswoman-Elect." During this transition period, new representatives-elect prepare to assume the duties of their new job, which include attending to constituent requests and concerns, obtaining desirable committee assignments (I will explain House committees in detail), and begin the process of drafting legislation. For a representative who has been reelected, the transition from candidate to officeholder is seamless, with no interruption in the carrying out of his or her official duties. At the beginning of the new year, all 435 representatives are sworn into office, and the new Congress begins its legislative work.

☆ 2: THE LEADERSHIP ☆

Who "runs" the House of Representatives? Generally speaking, the leadership of the majority party in the House makes decisions regarding which bills are voted on—and when they are voted on—as well as to which committees members are assigned. The elected leader of the House—and arguably its most powerful member—is the Speaker. Following the Speaker, in descending order of authority, are the Majority Leader and the Majority Whip, and the Conference/Caucus Chairman, and a number of deputy whips.

★ THE SPEAKER ★

Technically, the position of Speaker of the House is not a party leadership position. Indeed, all members of the House have the right to cast a vote for its Speaker. Thus, the Speaker—unlike all other leadership positions in the House—is elected by the entire legislative body. In this sense, the Speaker is not only the leader of his or her party in the House, but also the leader of the entire House. When the newly elected House of Representatives is sworn into office, an election for the Speakership is held.[1] While members of the House can cast a vote for virtually anyone for Speaker, the election usually comes down to two candidates, one from each party. Following the most recent election, which took place in 2012, the election for Speaker essentially came down to two members—Republican John Boehner and Democrat Nancy Pelosi. Despite some defections, the Republican majority in the House prevailed and Boehner was elected Speaker (a position he had held since 2011).[2]

In reality, the leader of the majority party is usually elected Speaker. Yet the U.S. Constitution does not describe the Speakership as a partisan position. In fact, the Constitution does not even require the Speaker to be an elected member of the House. Today, however, the Speakership is clearly a partisan leadership role, and members who are elected Speaker of the House tend to be committed partisans. This is logical when understood within the context of congressional party politics: in order to win an election for a leadership position within the House, a member must have strong support within his or her own party. Members gain such support from fellow members by being loyal soldiers for their parties. Thus, House members who are eventually elected to leadership positions generally have a record of party loyalty. A point of linguistic clarification may be in order here. One will often hear members of the House—particularly House leaders—refer to "the Democratic Caucus" and the "Republican Conference." While "caucuses" will be explained in greater detail later, it should be noted that the Democratic Caucus refers to the coalition of all Democratic members of the House. Thus, the term "Democratic Caucus" is effectively synonymous with "House Democrats." Republicans in the House refer to their coalition as a "conference," but the effective meaning is no different. The "House Republican Conference" refers to the coalition of all elected Republicans in the House. These terms will be used interchangeably in this book.

While the Speaker of the House exerts considerable influence over the chamber's legislative agenda (determining which bills will be voted on at specific times), he or she is often not a visible presence presiding over the House. In fact, the Speaker usually delegates the duties of presiding over House proceedings to other members. (The member presiding over the House is referred to as the "Speaker pro Tempore," or "Speaker for a time.") The Speaker's most significant constitutional role is perhaps that he or she is second in the line of presidential succession after the vice president. Thus, in the event of the tragic death of both the president and vice president, the Speaker would assume the presidency.

While the position of Speaker of the House has long been inseparable from a party leadership role, the Speakership arguably became far more partisan following the Republican revolution of 1994 and the election of Newt Gingrich of Georgia as Speaker. Arguably, Gingrich governed the House like no previous Speaker. His personal style, political ambitions, and institutional vision amounted to a radical departure from tradition. In general, the Speaker of the House had not been regarded as a fitting position for a politician with truly national ambitions. Generally speaking, politicians who launch successful presidential campaigns must have a certain degree of personal charm and charisma. They are adept at giving television interviews, and make a favorable impression on voters with their looks, speaking style, and personal qualities. They must be a plausible and attractive public face of their political parties. Yet historically, the Speaker of the House must be a master of the "inside game." They are gifted deal-makers and negotiators, and operate largely behind the scenes. Their careers are steeped in the political history of the House as an institution, and they become creatures of the House of Representatives. For the most part, they deal in process rather than policy. For a person who fancies himself or herself a political visionary with an ambitious national policy agenda, the Speakership would likely be considered a mismatch.

The iconic contemporary Speakers of the House— such as Sam Rayburn and Tip O'Neill—were master legislators who could shepherd bills through the chamber under extraordinarily difficult circumstances. They were not, however, policy or political visionaries, and never aspired to be.

Gingrich, however, was a different animal. A hero to the conservative movement and a boogeyman to liberals, few American political figures have been more controversial or polarizing. To his supporters, he was brilliant, cunning, ambitious, intellectual, and a political visionary. To his critics, he was flamboyant, grandiose, egomaniacal, diabolical, and totally lacking an ethical or moral compass. Gingrich, for his part, certainly saw his election to the Speakership as a historic moment in American politics that portended nothing short of a political revolution. (In fact, the 1994 midterm election—in which Republicans gained 53 House seats, and wrested control of the chamber from the Democrats for the first time in four decades—became known (particularly among Republicans) as the "Republican Revolution."[3]

In some respects, Gingrich was an unlikely figure to lead a national conservative movement, having begun his political career in solidly moderate territory within the Republican Party. In 1968, Gingrich served as the southern regional director of the presidential campaign of New York Governor Nelson Rockefeller, an icon among Republican moderates and progressives (and who would later serve as Vice President under President Gerald Ford).[4]

In his first campaign for public office in 1974, Gingrich ran an energetic but ultimately unsuccessful campaign against Rep. John James "Jack" Flynt, a conservative Democrat associated with the segregationist "Dixiecrat" wing of the party. In the kickoff speech from his 1974 campaign, Gingrich took aim both at corporate interests and environmental activists, saying: "Greedy economic giants are raping the environment, polluting the water we drink and the air we breathe—yet all too often the reformers offer solutions that will lead to unemployment and economic chaos." During that same campaign, this statement by Gingrich reportedly led conservative icon and former Republican presidential candidate Barry Goldwater to consider withdrawing his endorsement of Gingrich: "Today, the American oil industry is receiving windfall profits while the American people are paying through their noses for home heating oil and gasoline."[5] These statements differ dramatically in both tone and substance from the rhetoric Gingrich would employ in his later years. The politics of the American South were in the midst of a transformation during Gingrich's rise to power, and his own political evolution prepared him well to take the reins of a Republican party that was establishing its power base in the old Confederacy.

Although Gingrich fell short in his first campaign—and then lost narrowly again to Flynt in 1976—he ran for the seat for a third consecutive time when the incumbent Democrat retired in 1978. This time, Gingrich prevailed, and soon established himself as a conservative firebrand in the House.[6] He formed the Conservative Opportunity Society, a coalition of like-minded, activist GOP members in the House who pushed for a far more aggressive approach to challenging the Democratic leadership, whose decades-long grip on the House had continued uninterrupted and relatively unchallenged.[7]

A major milestone in Gingrich's rise to prominence came in 1984, when he found himself engaged in a heated confrontation with House Majority Leader Jim Wright (D-TX) and with Speaker Tip O'Neill during televised proceedings. Gingrich, who was then still a relatively junior member, had taken to giving speeches in front of an empty House chamber in which he excoriated Democratic members. (Late at night, members of the House may give what are known as "special orders" speeches on any topic of their choosing.) Specifically, he lit into ten House Democrats who had written a letter to Nicaraguan dictator Daniel Ortega. (In the letter, those Democratic members had urged Ortega to hold democratic elections.) Gingrich went as far as to argue that the authors of the letter could be prosecuted under the Logan Act, which prohibits unauthorized persons from engaging in diplomacy on behalf of the United States. He had accused one Democratic member of placing "Communist propaganda" in the Speaker's lobby. Yet no one watching Gingrich's broadsides, however, would have known that the Georgia Republican was speaking to an empty House chamber; the C-Span cameras never showed the empty seats before which Gingrich stood. Thus, it appeared as though Gingrich's charges had gone unanswered.

Democratic leaders were furious, and came to the House floor to confront Gingrich. A visibly angry Jim Wright—who was then the House Majority Leader—questioned whether Gingrich had the courage to repeat his accusations in the presence of the members whose patriotism he had attacked: "He's willing to engage in debate when members are not here—whose patriotism he's impugned. Is he not willing to engage in debate when we are here? Now that is the question!"

O'Neill was even more direct. Speaking directly to Gingrich, the Speaker thundered: "My personal opinion is this: you deliberately stood in that well before an empty House, and challenged these people, and challenged their patriotism, and it is the lowest thing that I've ever seen in my 32 years in Congress."

O'Neill's characterization of Gingrich's behavior as "lowest" violated House rules, which hold that members' remarks may not descend to personality. Rep. Trent Lott (R-MS)—a man who was perhaps more well-known for his tenure as Senate Majority Leader—rose to make an official procedural objection. He demanded that the Speaker's remarks "be taken down."[8] When a member's words are taken down, which occurs when his or her remarks are found to have violated House rules, that individual's remarks are literally stricken from the *Congressional Record*. In the transcript that will be published the following day, the words that were "taken down" will appear nowhere—as if they were never said. Yet there is an additional, highly putative consequence of having one's words taken down: the offending member is banned from speaking from the House floor for the rest of the day. When O'Neill's words were taken down, he became the first Speaker to receive such a reprimand in nearly two centuries.[9] (It should be noted, however, that following the House's reprimand of O'Neill, Lott asked the House to restore his speaking rights by unanimous consent.*)

For a complete list of former Speakers of the House, please see Appendix A.

★ THE MAJORITY LEADER ★

The two parties' leadership structures are not identical; however, when one party transitions from minority status to majority status (or vice versa), this necessitates changes in leadership. The #1 ranking member of the majority party—whether it is the Democrats or the Republicans who control the House—is, effectively, the Speaker. The #2 ranking member of the House majority is the "Majority Leader." As the position of "House Majority Leader" is not constitutionally defined, his or her role in the legislative process is fluid and subject to the leadership style of the Speaker. In other words, his or her political influence depends on the Speaker's

---

* A unanimous consent agreement literally refers to an arrangement technically agreed upon by all members of the body. Thus, when one member makes a unanimous consent request, any member of the House may object.

willingness to delegate responsibilities and relinquish personal power. Under Speaker Dennis Hastert, for example, a Republican who was known for a low-key personal style and who did not relish the limelight, House Majority Leader Tom DeLay took on a more prominent role in the Republican leadership. This was in marked contrast to the tenure of Speaker Nancy Pelosi, who has been referred to by some political observers as one of the most powerful Speakers in history.[10] (She was also known to have a frosty personal relationship with the #2 ranking House Democrat, Steny Hoyer of Maryland.[11]) Thus, during her time as speaker, Pelosi was regarded as the House Democrats' unequivocal leader. During Hastert's reign, however, political power within the Republican leadership seemed to be more diffuse.

Broadly speaking, the House Majority Leader is the Speaker's 2nd in command, and serves as the "floor leader" for the majority party. His or her most practical responsibility concerns scheduling legislation for consideration by the House. Thus, the Majority Leader plays a key role in setting the House's legislative agenda. Still, managing the day-to-day tasks of the legislative calendar is a duty that he or she carries out in consultation with other members of the leadership. For example, the Majority Leader would be highly unlikely to schedule a bill to be voted on by the House if the Speaker strongly opposed it.

★ THE MAJORITY WHIP ★

The Whip, the 3rd ranking member of the majority party in the House, is charged with enforcing party unity. The term stems from the phrase "whipping in," in which a hunter prevents dogs from straying too far from the pack, and this task accurately describes the chief responsibility of the Whip in a political context. Although the Whip delegates actual vote-counting duties to a deputy, he or she generally must have an accurate sense of where his or her members stand on a particular bill. The Whip strives to persuade members of his or her caucus or conference to vote in accordance with the leadership's wishes. Such persuasion can involve both mild and heavy-handed tactics, and the process of "whipping a vote" can sometimes be an ugly one, particularly when the leadership is struggling to line up the votes required to pass an important bill.

One such vote, which has become rather infamous among political observers, concerned a 2003 bill to add a prescription drug benefit to Medicare, the federal health insurance program for the elderly. The bill was a major priority for President George W. Bush, who saw it as a critical component of his domestic policy agenda. Garnering enough votes to pass the bill proved to be a herculean task for House Republicans, who held a narrow majority in the chamber. The bill faced opposition from Democrats, who objected for the new role carved out for private health plans (known as "Medicare Advantage" plans) in the program. A coalition of conservative Republicans, meanwhile, objected to expanding the Medicare program to include prescription drug coverage—a policy goal that they viewed antithetical to conservative principles. Thus, House conservatives had staged a revolt against their party's leadership and made an all-out effort—aided by opposition to the bill among Democrats—to kill the legislation. When the bill came up for a vote, it appeared to be headed for a stinging defeat. Seeking to avoid being humiliated on the House floor—and to prevent President Bush's signature domestic policy proposal from being defeated in chamber controlled by his own party—the Republican leadership launched an effort to persuade opponents of the bill to change their votes. What ensued on the floor of the House was one of the most heated and chaotic scenes in legislative history.

The vote, which took place on November 22, 2003, began at 3:00 a.m. While Congress regularly conducts legislative business late into the evening, holding a vote on such a major item was highly unusual. As House members began to cast their votes, it became clear that the bill was in trouble. After fifteen minutes—the standard time allotted to votes in the House (although this time limit is not strictly enforced)—the bill appeared poised to fail by a vote of 216–218. Unwilling to accept defeat, GOP leaders held the vote open for *three hours* as they cornered Republican members (and a handful of Democrats) who had voted against the bill. Further adding to the drama (and outrage) surrounding the vote, Republicans took the extraordinary step of stopping the C-Span cameras so that the public could not observe the machinations involved to pressure members into changing their votes. (C-Span is a cable network that covers virtually all activity on the House and Senate floor live on television.) After considerable arm-twisting, three Republicans and three Democrats changed their votes, enabling the bill to pass by a 220–215 margin.[12]

Then-House Majority Leader Tom DeLay (R-TX), a former Whip himself, played a critical role in that vote—and one that led to his being publicly admonished by the House Ethics Committee. During the vote, one of the Republican members who had been the recipient of some of the most ferocious pressure from party leaders was then-Rep. Nick Smith of Michigan, who was retiring from Congress. DeLay had promised Smith that he would help to pave the way for his son to replace him in the upcoming election if he supported the Medicare drug bill. Such a quid pro quo explicitly violates House rules, and DeLay was thus reprimanded.[13]

★ THE DEPUTIES ★

While the House Majority Whip is the individual "in charge" of the majority party's whipping operation, he or she has a number of deputy whips who assist in carrying out the duties associated with vote counting. Each party's deputy whips are led by a "chief deputy," who serves as the assistant to the Whip. The chief deputy whip is the person responsible for vote counting, a critical component of a party's whipping operation. The Republican Chief Deputy Whip is currently Rep. Peter Roskam (R-IL).[14] The Democrats, meanwhile, use a slightly different nomenclature to describe their whipping leadership structure, which can only be described as gratuitously confusing. Essentially, the Democrats call all of their deputy whips "chief deputy whips," and refer to the leader of the chief deputy whips with the title of "Senior Chief Deputy Whip." Since 2011, this role is currently filled by Rep. John Lewis, a longtime representative from Georgia and icon of the civil rights movement.[15]

While deputy whips are not well known to the public and do not receive nearly as much media attention as more senior leaders, they can occasionally catapult to prominence. Such was the case with former Rep. Dennis Hastert (R-IL), who was serving as the Republican Chief Deputy Whip in the late 1990s when a series of scandals upended the Republican leadership, and thus elevated him all the way to the Speakership. Following the 1998 midterm elections, Speaker Newt Gingrich (R-GA) faced a rebellion from his conference. The Republicans had lost five House seats, an unusually poor showing in a midterm election for a party that does not control the White House. (Usually, the party "out of power" in the White House gains seats in midterm elections.) Republican members, who had grown weary of his leadership style and felt that he had badly mishandled the impeachment of President Clinton, were ready for the conservative firebrand to make his exit off the national stage.

To replace Gingrich, Republicans—who, despite losses, had maintained their majority in the House—chose Rep. Robert Livingston of Louisiana. Livingston, then the chairman of the powerful Appropriations Committee (which will be addressed in the chapter outlining the committee system in the House), was well liked by members of his conference and seemed like a logical choice for Speaker. Before he could assume his new role, however, *Hustler* magazine published details of Livingston's extramarital affairs, which he had carried out while attacking Clinton for carrying on an affair with Monica Lewinsky. This left Livingston open to charges of hypocrisy. He announced that he would not pursue the Speakership, and promptly resigned from his seat in Congress.[16]

Tom DeLay, then the Majority Whip, was seen as too controversial a figure to serve as Speaker of a bitterly divided House. Rep. Dick Armey, who was serving as the Majority Leader, had just survived a fierce challenge from Rep. Steve Largent (R-OK) for the Majority Leader's post.[17] In desperation, the Republicans turned to Hastert, a mild-mannered, low-key representative who had been known as something of a "backbencher" in the House.[18] Thus, Hastert rose from being an obscure chief deputy whip all the way to Speaker of the House.

★ MINORITY PARTY LEADERSHIP ★

When the majority party loses control of the House of Representatives and assumes minority status, its leadership structure necessarily changes. Since the Speakership is effectively the exclusive prerogative of the majority party, the newly minted minority party in the House essentially loses a leadership position. Thus, one member of the party's leadership loses his or her job, and soon becomes a rank-and-file member without a leadership title.

In 2011, however, the Democrats found a novel way to circumvent a process that ends with one member being pushed out of the leadership: they simply added a new leadership position. After the Democrats lost control of the House following the 2010 elections, the party held new elections. Democratic members quickly rallied around Pelosi as their party leader, which ensured that she would become the Minority Leader in the House. Steny Hoyer (D-MD), who was the #2 Democrat and had thus served as House Majority Leader during the party's four years of running the chamber, was assumed to be in line for the position of Minority Whip (the #2 leadership position for the minority party in the House). This left Rep. James Clyburn (D-SC), in the position of being demoted. Clyburn, the highest-ranking African American in the House, had previously served as Caucus Chairman in 2006 before the Democrats won back the House. At that time, since the Democrats were in the minority, the caucus chairmanship was the #3 leadership position for House Democrats. Following the Democratic wave of 2006, in which Democrats became the majority party in the House for the first time in twelve years, Clyburn retained his spot as the #3 Democrat in the House. Since the Democrats were now in the majority, Clyburn became the Majority Whip. After the Democrats lost the House in 2010, however, he made it clear that he had no intention of returning to the position of Caucus Chairman and threatened to run against Hoyer for the position of Minority Whip. Seeking to avoid an intraparty feud and prevent a member from being effectively booted from the leadership, the

Democrats invented a new title—that of "Assistant Democratic Leader." Clyburn was elected to this post, and Hoyer retained his status as the #2 House Democrat in the role of Minority Whip.[19]

In addition, when one party loses control of the House of Representatives, a shakeup in its leadership frequently takes place following the election. When the Republicans lost control of the House following the 2006 midterm elections, Speaker J. Dennis Hastert had been reelected to his Illinois Congressional seat. Given the Republicans' poor showing, however, he stepped down from the leadership altogether, and later resigned his seat in Congress.[20]

Although Hastert's disappearance from national politics was certainly noteworthy, an even more dramatic shakeup within the Republican leadership had already taken place months earlier when it had become clear that the GOP was in serious trouble. Back in February of 2006, it was clear that a wave of voter discontentment with Republican governance posed a considerable threat to the party's efforts to retain control of Congress. House Majority Leader Tom DeLay had been forced to resign in disgrace, as he was facing criminal charges pertaining to money laundering and campaign finance law violations. (Although he was found guilty of money laundering, DeLay's conviction was later overturned.) DeLay's resignation created a power vacuum that gave rise to a hard-fought race to replace DeLay as Majority Leader. Rep. Roy Blunt (R-MO), who was serving as Majority Whip at the time of DeLay's resignation, stepped in to become "acting Majority Leader" on an interim basis. Yet when the House Republicans held an election for the Majority Leader's post, Blunt was challenged by Rep. John Boehner, the Chairman of the Education and Workforce Committee. In a major upset, Boehner prevailed. His victory was indicative of House Republicans' dissatisfaction with their leadership, and their skittishness about the upcoming election.[21]

For Boehner personally, his victory amounted not only to a remarkable political resurrection. After having served as Republican Conference Chairman under Newt Gingrich's Speakership, he was ousted from his leadership post following his party's poor showing in the 1998 midterm elections. Thus, his election to Majority Leader marked the beginning of a political comeback. After the Republicans lost control of Congress in 2006, Boehner was elected Minority Leader. Blunt, meanwhile, was elected Minority Whip, serving as the #2 Republican behind the man who had defeated him nine months earlier. When the GOP regained control of the House in 2011, Boehner was elected Speaker, thereby cementing his political comeback.[22] Blunt—Boehner's former vanquished rival—also enjoyed his own political comeback as he was elected to the U.S. Senate in 2010.[23]

With the Democrats in control of the U.S. Senate during the first six years of the Obama presidency, Speaker Boehner was effectively the most powerful Republican in the country, and President Obama's chief opponent in Washington. Unlike in the U.S. Senate, the majority party's leadership in the House has almost complete control over what legislation is voted on in the chamber. In essence, Speaker Boehner—with the support of the rest of the House GOP leadership—could block President Obama's agenda from seeing the light of day in the House of Representatives. For the most part, this was precisely what transpired. The Democratic leadership in the Senate has sought to advance Obama's policy goals, while House Republicans pursued their own agenda. This is a direct result of the 2012 elections, in which Obama was reelected by a relatively comfortable margin, Democrats retained their majority in the Senate, and Republicans kept control of the House.[24] The result was political gridlock, in which little or no progress is made on major issues facing the country.

A NATIONAL LEADER WITH ★ A LOCAL CONSTITUENCY: THE DUAL TASK ★ OF CONGRESSIONAL LEADERSHIP

Although congressional leaders enjoy national political stature, their constituents are confined to the congressional districts from which they are elected. Maintaining a leadership role while attending to the needs and sentiments of one's district can be a difficult balancing act indeed, and some notable House figures have found themselves out of a job when the voters of their districts determined that those members no longer represented their interests. In 1994, Speaker Tom Foley lost his seat in the Republican wave that returned control of Congress to Republicans for the first time in four decades. Foley, a liberal Democrat who had represented his Eastern Washington State district since 1964, became the first Speaker to lose a reelection bid in more than 130 years.[25] Foley's district, which had long been politically competitive, had begun to develop a Republican lean. Given the Democrats' unpopularity in 1994, conditions were ripe for a major upset.

In 2014, House Majority Leader Eric Cantor (R-VA) became the first member holding that position to lose his seat in a primary. His stunning defeat, which caused a political earthquake in Washington, D.C., was a remarkable political upset. During the primary campaign, Cantor had out-fundraised his challenger by a ratio of 26 to 1. In fact, his campaign had spent more money at steak houses than his opponent had spent on his entire campaign.[26] In essence, he seemed to have simply been caught completely flat-footed.

At the start of the 2014 midterm election season, Cantor was widely viewed the heavy favorite to succeed

John Boehner as Speaker, who seemed likely to step down after that year's midterm elections. In preparing for his political ascent, Cantor spent much of the primary season raising money and campaigning for other members, thus building a network of support for an expected bid for the Speakership. In doing so, he neglected his own reelection, and was slow to recognize an unexpectedly strong challenge from Dave Brat, an ultraconservative Tea Party Republican and college professor whom very few people in Washington had ever heard of.[27] Ironically, Eric Cantor was known as a brash, hard-line conservative who played a role in fueling the Tea Party's rise to dominance over the House's Republican conference. In essence, Cantor's career was brought down by the very political movement he had hoped would enable him to become Speaker.

★ ELECTION TO THE LEADERSHIP ★

Intraparty elections for leadership posts are sometimes framed by candidates and observers as determining the future of the two political parties in Congress. Such analysis may often be hyperbolic, but they can indisputably be harbingers of important political trends. As described earlier, John Boehner's surprise victory over then-Rep. Roy Blunt (R-MO) in the race for Majority Leader in 2006 signaled growing unease among rank-

and-file Republicans with their leadership amid the
threat of a Democratic wave in 2006. In 2001, the race
for minority whip pitted Rep. Nancy Pelosi, who represents an ultraliberal San Francisco–based district,
against Rep. Steny Hoyer, who represents a more moderate and suburban district in Maryland. Pelosi's win
was described as a victory for the party's liberal wing.

Following a leadership race, both candidates generally work to mend fences politically and emphasize
that which unites rather than divides their political
party. After the legendary Rep. Morris ("Mo") Udall,
a liberal giant who represented an Arizona congressional district for thirty years, lost a race for Majority
Leader to Rep. Hale Boggs (D-LA) Udall reportedly
ended his concession speech by turning his "MO" but-
ton upside down so that it read "OW."[28]

★ THE PRESIDENT AND THE SPEAKER: ★
PAST AND PRESENT

While gridlock may be the norm in political climate
during the Obama presidency, this was not always the
case. One need not look far in the distant past to find
examples of a more cooperative (and productive) divided
government. In fact, the early days of the Reagan era
provide an illustrative example of a very different political climate. Now, this point can be overstated. The

Reagan era—in which Democrats remained in control of the House—was surely characterized by partisanship, squabbles, negative attacks, etc. Yet one would need only to look at the example of his sweeping tax cuts—which amounted to his signature domestic policy initiative—to see that his relationship with Speaker Tip O'Neill was dramatically different from Obama's relationship with Boehner. To be sure, Reagan's friendship with O'Neill has been exaggerated and with time has become the stuff of legend. They were rivals, not allies. And they fought bitterly over policy. O'Neill was particularly outraged by Reagan's tax proposal, which overwhelmingly favored wealthier taxpayers. He opposed the bill, as did most liberal Democrats in the House. He did, however, allow for a vote on the tax bill.[29]

Why did O'Neill—along with the rest of the Democratic House leadership—agree to hold a vote on Reagan's tax proposal, rather than effectively kill it by denying the bill a vote on the House floor? Perhaps pressure from conservative Democrats was a factor. Yet reporter Gloria Borger wrote in *U.S. News & World Report* that O'Neill felt "the president should be given a chance to pass his programs, given his impressive victory [in the 1980 presidential election]. . . . Tip took a pounding from his liberal flank, but he was determined to let Reagan have his votes on his tax cuts. This, of course, was not done without some political consideration. 'Give him enough rope,' Tip used to confide to journalists like me. He was convinced that Reagan would hand the Democrats a platform to run on in 1982."[30]

Moreover, following the vote—in which, in a major blow to Democrats, the House passed Reagan's tax bill—Democratic leaders called Reagan in front of the press to congratulate him on his political victory. Rep. Dan Rostenkowski, who was then serving as the chairman of the tax-writing committee in the House—and who opposed Reagan's 1981 tax bill—told Reagan: "Well, Mr. President, you're tough . . . You beat us. . . . It means you're working at your job."[31]

While O'Neill believed that votes held on Reagan's tax cuts could be a boon to the party's efforts in the 1982 midterm elections, he also felt the president had earned the chance to put his agenda before Congress. By today's standards, such deference by the Speaker to a president of an opposing party would be unfathomable. Indeed, this would be akin to Speaker Boehner agreeing to hold a vote on Obama's signature health-care reform law (if Boehner had been Speaker at the time).

3: THE RULES COMMITTEE

While the next chapter will explain the functions and importance of the various House committees, I have devoted an entire chapter to the Rules Committee because its importance and unique legislative role warrants such attention.

The House Rules Committee—formally known as the "Committee on Rules"—plays a critical role in how the institution operates as a legislative body. It is often referred to as the House's "traffic cop," which is perhaps an apt description of its essential function.

For all intents and purposes, there are only two ways a bill can be brought up for debate and voted on in the House. First, it can be brought up for debate as required by a "rule" passed by the Rules Committee. Second, it can be brought up by the House leadership under a process known as "suspension of the rules." Under the latter procedure, a bill must receive a two-thirds majority vote to pass. Thus, bills are generally only brought up under suspension of the rules if they are noncontroversial (such as measures to rename post offices). Most bills of substance and consequence reach the House floor by way of the powerful Rules Committee.*

The Rules Committee enables the leadership of the majority party in the House to tightly control the manner in which legislation is debated, amended, and voted in the chamber. The committee's central function is to write "rules" that govern debate on major legislation. Before a bill cleared by the Rules Committee can be debated, the House must first pass the rule that accompanies the bill. Each rule dictates how much time is allotted for debate on the bill; which amendments, if any, may be offered; and the time permitted for debate on each amendment. In fact, a rule can even amend the bill before it reaches the House floor. (This is known as a "self-executing" rule—the changes made by the rule to the bill take effect automatically when the House passes the rule.) With respect to amendments, there are three kinds of rules: open, closed, and structured.

---

* There have been exceptions to this general practice. Sometimes, the House leadership will bring up a bill under suspension of the rules if it has broad, bipartisan support—such as a bill to fund defense or veterans' programs.

An open rule allows for an unlimited number of amendments. A closed rule permits no amendments whatsoever. A structured rule allows for a limited number of amendments.

Clearly, a committee with such sweeping authority over "floor debate" on legislation is a powerful one. ("Floor debate," a term used throughout this book, simply refers to any debate on a measure that takes place on the House floor.) Yet it is the Rules Committee's membership structure that makes it such a powerful tool for the majority party's leadership. On all other committees, the ratio of majority party members to minority party members roughly mirrors that of the makeup of the full House. This is not the case on the Rules Committee. On this committee, the majority party enjoys a 9–4 advantage over the minority party. Thus, the minority on the Rules Committee is effectively powerless to exert influence over the committee's deliberations. Moreover, each party's leadership appoints their caucus or conference's most loyal partisan members to the Rules Committee, which makes defections on the committee exceedingly rare. For the reasons described in the paragraphs above, the House Rules Committee enables the majority party to enjoy a degree of control over the chamber's legislative business that a Senate Majority Leader could only dream of. While the Senate has a "Rules and Administration Committee," it does not serve a similar function to the

House Committee on Rules. Indeed, the Rules Committee is a distinguishing feature of the House, and appreciating its influence over the business of the House is critical to understanding the legislative process.

Although the majority party's control over the Rules Committee is nearly absolute, this was not always the case. Indeed, the degree to which the modern Rules Committee functions as an arm of the majority party's leadership reflects major institutional and cultural changes that have reshaped the House of Representatives since the early 1960s. Until a revolt by liberal insurgents disempowered Howard Smith, a Virginia Democrat and segregationist, in his role as chairman of the Rules Committee in 1961, Smith was effectively an autonomous political actor. As will be further explained in the chapter on congressional committees, committee chairmen generally were far more powerful during the New Deal and civil rights eras than they are today. The House leadership's control over the Rules Committee is particularly critical, however, because it enables the Speaker and his or her lieutenants to dictate the chamber's day-to-day legislative agenda.

Given the role that the Rules Committee plays in carrying out the legislative will of the House's governing leadership, the committee's chairman tends to be a reliable supporter of his or her leadership. (Some observers would, in fact, regard the Rules Committee chair as a de facto member of the leadership.) From

2011 to 2015, the Rules Committee Chairman was Rep. Pete Sessions (R-TX), a close ally of Speaker John Boehner. From 2007 to 2011, the Rules Committee was chaired by Rep. Louise Slaughter (D-NY), a staunch ally of Minority Leader (and former Speaker) Nancy Pelosi.

In an illustration of the outsized role the Rules Committee can play in legislative debates, Slaughter briefly became a lightning rod during the eleventh hour of an ultimately successful Democratic effort to pass a comprehensive health-care reform bill. A colorful figure who has long represented a congressional district in upstate New York but who speaks with the twang of her native Kentucky, Slaughter had considerable experience tangling with her Republican counterparts during debate in her committee and on the House floor. Yet when Democrats found themselves scrambling to stave off a devastating legislative defeat of President Obama's signature domestic policy initiative, Slaughter proposed a parliamentary maneuver that—although it was never actually used in the passage of health-care reform legislation—created a firestorm of controversy.[1]

In essence, the Democrats found themselves in the following predicament: the House and Senate had initially passed different versions of a health-care overhaul, as is typical at the start of a legislative process. Senate Democrats had passed their bill with a "super majority" of 60 votes, the number of votes required to end a filibuster and allow a vote on final passage. (A "filibuster," a procedural tactic unique to the U.S. Senate, allows a single senator to debate a bill indefinitely, and can only be defeated with the support of 60 senators. Thus, the minority party in the Senate can block legislation with a minority of only 40 votes.)

Following passage of the Senate bill, Republican Scott Brown won a special election in Massachusetts to fill the Senate seat of the late Edward M. Kennedy, a liberal icon and key supporter of health-care reform. Brown's victory cost Senate Democrats their 60-vote supermajority, leaving them without the procedural math they had been counting on to vote on a final health-care reform that included changes demanded by House members. House Democrats insisted they would only pass the Senate's bill if Senate Democratic leaders promised to then pass a separate bill implementing changes sought by the House through a process known as budget reconciliation. Budget reconciliation measures can effectively be fast-tracked through the Senate and passed with 51 votes.

Many House liberals, however, regarded the Senate-passed bill as capitulation to moderate and conservative Democratic demands, and assailed its lack of a government-run insurance plan to compete with private insurers. Others objected to its tax on high-cost "Cadillac" insurance plans, as the tax had been vigorously opposed by labor unions, and was likely to be unpopular with key constituent groups. Yet many Democrats believed that the Senate-passed bill was preferable to passing no bill at all, and still held out hope that changes favored by progressives could be implemented through the reconciliation process. In order to assuage the concerns of House Democrats threatening to balk at passing the Senate health-care bill, Slaughter proposed that the House vote on a self-executing rule (see explanation above) that would "deem" the Senate bill passed when the House passed the rule. In other words, when the House passed the self-executing rule for debate on the Senate bill, the bill itself would be "deemed passed." This essentially allowed the House to pass the Senate bill without voting on it directly. This strategy became known as "Deem and Pass," or "the Slaughter Solution."[2] Republicans, in an effort to portray the maneuver as undemocratic, corrupt, and diabolical, preferred to dub the plan as the "Slaughter House Rules" and "Demon Pass."[3]

While the wisdom of this strategy was questioned by many political observers (including some liberals), it was in reality a parliamentary tactic employed many times in the past, more frequently by Republicans than Democrats. Still, the uproar over the Slaughter Solution threatened to derail a delicate effort to pass an increasingly imperiled health-care bill, and Democratic leaders ultimately abandoned the plan. In the end, the House passed the Senate bill with a clear-cut vote, and both chambers passed changes sought by the House through budget reconciliation. The legislative process that resulted in the Affordable Care Act becoming law in 2010 will be outlined in greater detail as a case study later in this book.

During the Bush and Obama administrations, the increasingly partisan and caustic nature of the politics of the House has been very much on display in the Rules Committee, and in floor debate on the rules that it crafts for consideration of bills by the full House. When the Democrats launched a spirited and ultimately successful effort to regain control of the House during the 2006 midterm election campaign, they vowed a more open and egalitarian process for debating bills. Among their proposed reforms was a general policy of providing open and structured rules that would allow for open debate and the offering of amendments to legislation. Although they initially made good on this campaign promise, the era of openness in the House under Democratic control admittedly proved short-lived. By the end of 2008, the Rules Committee was sharply restricting Republican efforts to offer amendments during legislative debates.[4] Democratic leaders argued that Republicans had used obstructionist parliamentary tactics to an unprecedented degree and threatened to leave the House unable to carry out its business.

Disputes over amendments proved particularly toxic during debates over appropriations bills, which provide funding for government services and operations, including social welfare programs and the military. Traditionally, appropriations bills were debated under open rules, with members offering unlimited amendments. Consideration of such bills was time-consuming, but the bill's "floor manager" (the member, generally from the majority party, who is charged with coordinating debate on legislation) would eventually reach an agreement with his or her counterpart from the minority party to limit further amendments to a number and variety that were agreeable to both parties. While Democrats accused Republicans of engaging in dilatory tactics, Republicans protested that debate on amendments was being shut down prematurely and that the Democrats had entertained debate on very few amendments by historical standards.[5]

Regardless, a pattern clearly emerges when one examines how House majorities have governed over the last decade. When the minority party is seeking to regain control of the House, its members promise a return to a more open legislative process. Once in power—and charged with the responsibility of governing—the majority closes down the chamber's legislative proceedings in order to further its political and policy agenda. Despite the Republicans' promises in 2010 to restore a more open amendment process in the House, 2013 was a year marked by a record forty-four closed rules, leading Democrats to accuse the Republican majority of running the "most closed congress in history."[6]

4: STANDING COMMITTEES

The twenty standing committees of the House of Representatives effectively have legislative jurisdiction over specific areas of public policy. These committees hold hearings and consider bills relating to these policy areas, and thus play a major role in the process that culminates in a bill ultimately being signed into law by the president. After a bill is introduced in the House, it is referred to the appropriate standing committee. A bill relating to energy policy, for example, would be referred to the Energy and Commerce Committee. A bill pertaining to farm subsidies, however, would be referred to the Agriculture Committee. Committees consider bills under their jurisdiction in a legislative process known as a "markup." During markups, committee members can offer amendments to the underlying legislation being considered. When the committee has concluded its consideration of a bill, it holds a vote on whether to pass the measure out of committee, or in the language of House legislative procedures, it votes to "report" the bill to the full House.

Sometimes, a bill's provisions will affect public policies overseen by multiple committees, and therefore will be subject to review by each of those committees before reaching the House floor for debate, amendments, and a vote on final passage. President Obama's health-care law (the Affordable Care Act), for example, made sweeping changes to current law concerning health policy. However, it also made changes to tax law through its imposition of a tax on high-cost insurance plans, and by providing tax credits to help low- and middle-income Americans purchase insurance. In addition, it imposed new requirements on employers, mandating that those with more than fifty employees provide health insurance to their workers or pay a fine. Thus, the Affordable Care Act was amended by the Energy and Commerce Committee (which has jurisdiction over health policy), the Education and Labor Committee, and the Ways and Means Committee (which has jurisdiction over tax legislation).

The chairman of each committee is a member of the majority party, while his or her counterpart from the minority is known as the "ranking member." Republicans, after winning control of the House in 1994, instituted term limits for their committee chairmen. After three two-year terms, their chairmen are required to step down. Provided that they enjoy sufficient seniority, they may then have the opportunity to chair a different committee. Historically, Democrats have not imposed term limits on chairmanships when they have controlled the House.

When control of the House changes hands, the change in leadership is also reflected at the committee level. When Democrats lost control of the House following the 2010 midterm elections, for example, Republicans were also guaranteed a majority as well as the chairmanships of House committees. This meant that some Democratic members with little seniority lost their seats on those committees altogether.

Other, less consequential but nonetheless noteworthy changes also occur following one party's takeover of the chamber. Until the Democrats lost control of the House in 1994, and once again during the four-year period in which they controlled the chamber from 2007 to 2011, the committee with jurisdiction over education and labor issues was known as the "Education and Labor Committee." This was the title given to the standing committee when it was first established in 1867.[1] When Republicans took over the House in 1995, they renamed it the "Committee on Economic and Educational Opportunities." In 2011, they changed the name of the committee from "Education and Labor" to "Education and the Workforce." This change reflected political and cultural differences between the two parties with regards to organized labor and workplace regulations. (Democrats have long been the party allied with labor unions and in favor of greater workplace protections, while Republicans, who view workplace regulations as placing an onerous burden on business, have had an antagonistic relationship with organized labor.) In 1995, the newly elected Republican majority also renamed the "Natural Resources Committee" to remove the word "natural." In addition, the Foreign Affairs Committee was renamed the "International Relations Committee." Upon regaining control of the House in 2006, the Democrats changed the committees' titles to what they had been prior to Republican control.[2]

Often, when the House majority and minority parties trade places following an election, the ranking member of a committee becomes its chairman, and vice versa. The ranking member, however, is by no means guaranteed a committee chairmanship should his or her party take over the House. In 2007, after the Democrats wrested control of the House from Republicans, the Energy and Commerce Committee's ranking Democrat, John D. Dingell, did indeed become its chairman. This change actually amounted to a triumphant return to the throne for Dingell, a Michigan Democrat who had served in the House for half a century. (Dingell is retiring at the end of the current session in 2015, after having served for roughly sixty years.) Before the Democrats' forty-year grip on the House came to an end in 1995, Dingell had become famous (his critics might say infamous) for the manner in which he conducted his committee's business, particularly the treatment of witnesses who testified at its hearings.

While Dingell is an unabashed liberal on many economic issues (he has long championed single-payer health care and expanded protections for workers), he was more conservative than many in his party on issues pertaining to environmental protection regulations. Although he has taken a more liberal position on some environmental issues, he has historically opposed efforts to impose more stringent fuel efficiency standards on automobiles. His record in this regard is hardly surprising as he represents a congressional district based in the suburbs of Detroit, where car manufacturing is a major industry and employer.

Dingell's stance on environmental regulation ultimately cost him his chairmanship after the election of Barack Obama as president in 2008. Following Obama's election, which coincided with the Democrats achieving larger majorities in the House and Senate than they had enjoyed following the 2006 midterm elections, the prospects for sweeping legislation to address global warming seemed brighter than they had ever been. House liberals, however, did not trust Dingell to take the helm of the committee charged with addressing the issue.

Rep. Henry Waxman, a California Democrat and staunch environmentalist, challenged Dingell for the chairmanship of the committee. The contest reflected the tension between labor and environmentalists, two key Democratic constituencies. Dingell represented the old-school New Deal Democratic tradition strongly associated with the labor movement. Although Waxman was also widely regarded as a liberal on labor issues (including supporting increases in the minimum wage and regulations intended to protect workers from exploitation), he represented a more contemporary liberal political tradition that, while certainly friendly to labor, emphasized a commitment to environmental protection. By a vote of 137–122, House Democrats chose Waxman as their Energy and Commerce Committee chairman.[3] Although the vote effectively relegated Dingell to rank-and-file status as a member of the committee, he was given the title "Chairman Emeritus" in an effort to acknowledge his decades of service on the committee.

Although seniority is often the overriding factor in determining committee chairmanships, the member with the most seniority on his or her committee is sometimes passed over for the chairman's job. In the example described above, Dingell, as the longest-ever serving member of the House, had seniority over

Waxman. The Democratic caucus chose Waxman in the hope that doing so would spur more dramatic action on environmental legislation, particularly a bill to address global warming. Yet there are other examples of members being passed over for chairmanships despite their seniority.

Former Rep. Jim Leach (R-IA) served in the House for a total of thirty years. During his tenure, Leach was in general a moderate-to-liberal Republican who, as a former Foreign Service officer, had considerable expertise on foreign affairs. Unlike most of his fellow House Republicans, however, who favored a hawkish foreign policy platform and viewed diplomacy and the United Nations in particular with suspicion, Leach was a devout internationalist and a skeptic of the use of military force. In 2001, Leach was the most senior member of the International Relations Committee (now called the Foreign Affairs Committee). Yet his party gave the chairman's gavel to Rep. Henry Hyde (R-IL). In addition to ensuring that the chairmanship of this committee was given to a more conservative member, offering the job to Hyde also helped to ensure that he did not retire and therefore force the Republicans to defend an open House seat. In 2005, when Republicans were preparing for Hyde to step down as chairman following the 2006 elections, Rep. Ileana Ros-Lehtinen (R-FL), whose conservative views on foreign policy were more closely aligned with those of the mainstream of her party, made it clear that she had every intention of challenging Leach for the post.[4] In the end, the question of Leach's candidacy to become chairman was a moot point; he was defeated for reelection by Dave Loebsack, a Democrat. Following his defeat, Leach endorsed then-Senator Barack Obama for president in 2008, and ultimately joined his administration as chairman of the National Endowment for the Humanities.[5]

When the Democrats won control of the House in the 2006 midterms, Rep. Jane Harman (D-CA) may have seemed like a logical choice to become chairman of the House Intelligence Committee, where she had served as the ranking Democrats since 2003. Harman, a moderate Democrat, had a decidedly frosty relationship with the more liberal Nancy Pelosi, who believed that Harman had been insufficiently critical of the Bush administration's foreign policy. An outside lobbying effort to convince Pelosi of Harman's suitability for the job reportedly infuriated Pelosi, and further damaged Harman's prospects.[6] Once Democrats took the reins of the House in January 2007, the chairmanship of the Intelligence Committee was instead given to Rep. Silvestre Reyes (D-TX).[7]

In what was at the time a highly unusual challenge to the seniority system, Rep. David Obey (D-WI), who represented a staunchly progressive Midwestern tradition epitomized by "Fighting Bob" La Follette—a former congressman, governor, and senator from

Wisconsin—challenged Neal Smith for the chairman-ship of the Appropriations Committee in 1994. Smith had been slated to succeed the ailing Rep. Bill Natcher (D-KY) as chairman. In making his case to his fellow House Democrats, Obey contended that Smith, while a decent and a loyal Democrat, was ill-equipped to handle the coming onslaught from Newt Gingrich and his band of fiery conservative insurgents. Obey was aided in his campaign for chairman by a number of House liber-als who would later ascend to top leadership posts, in-cluding Rep. Nancy Pelosi (D-CA) (the future Speaker) and Rep. Rosa DeLauro (D-CT).[8]

House committees also have subcommittees, which further specialize in certain legislative and policy ar-eas. For example, the Energy and Commerce Commit-tee has a subcommittee on Energy and Power, another on Health, and another on Commerce, Manufacturing, and Trade. A subcommittee will sometimes consider and report a bill before it goes to the full committee to be amended and reported to the full House. Thus, a bill relating to health policy would likely begin in the Energy and Commerce Subcommittee on Health before heading to the full committee. See Appendix B for a full list of House committees and their sub-committees.

What follows is a brief summary of the House's standing committees, and the legislative and policy areas over which they have jurisdiction.

EDUCATION AND LABOR/EDUCATION AND THE WORKFORCE

The Education and Labor or Education and the Workforce (depending on whether Democrats or Republicans control the chamber) Committee deals with legislation pertaining to education policy, including federal aid to and standards imposed on public schools, as well as higher education policy; and labor law, including workplace safety regulations, employment discrimination, and the minimum wage.

★ NATURAL RESOURCES ★

The Natural Resources Committee's legislative area includes policy concerning public lands (including national parks), water projects, mining, Native American lands, as well as the federal government's relationship with Native American tribes.

★ ENERGY AND COMMERCE ★

The Energy and Commerce Committee arguably has the most expansive jurisdiction of any House committee. It deals with legislation relating to public health, consumer protection, interstate and international commerce, telecommunications, energy and environmental policy, and food and drug safety.

★ WAYS AND MEANS ★

The Ways and Means Committee considers legislation dealing with taxes, tariffs, trade agreements, unemployment insurance, and facets of the Social Security and Medicare programs that pertain to tax revenue. It is often referred to as the "tax-writing committee."

★ APPROPRIATIONS ★

The Appropriations Committee deals with legislation that actually enables the federal government to spend money in order to carry out its functions. For example, while the Energy and Commerce committee could report a bill to authorize $200 million to be spent on a new energy program, the Appropriations Committee would then report a bill to actually spend up to $200 million on that program. In this scenario, Energy and Commerce is what is known as the "authorizing committee," because it provides a legal authorization for the government to spend money on a given program. Even if an authorization bill becomes law, however, no money would actually be spent on this hypothetical energy program until legislation was passed to "appropriate," or spend, the authorized amount of money.

★ AGRICULTURE ★

The Agriculture Committee has jurisdiction over bills that deal with agriculture policy, particularly farm subsidies. This includes most legislation affecting the nation's food supply, particularly the meat and dairy industries, and producers of grain. The committee also deals with measures pertaining to federal farm inspections, agricultural research, and nutrition programs (such as the Supplemental Nutrition Assistance Program, or what used to be known as the Food Stamp program).

★ JUDICIARY COMMITTEE ★

The Judiciary Committee has authority over issues relating to criminal and civil judicial proceedings, the federal courts, civil liberties, immigration, and patents. Although members of this committee often have a law degree, a legal background is not a requirement to serve on this committee.

★ ARMED SERVICES ★

The Armed Services Committee is charged with considering legislation dealing with programs and functions carried out by the Department of Defense, as well as certain Energy Department programs pertaining to nuclear nonproliferation. The committee is highly influential in matters relating to military operations.

★ FOREIGN AFFAIRS ★

The Foreign Affairs Committee has jurisdiction over matters pertaining to diplomacy, international law, foreign assistance programs, State Department functions, the United States Agency for International Development, and the enforcement of sanctions.

★ FINANCIAL SERVICES ★

The Financial Services Committee has authority over matters pertaining to banking, housing programs, securities, credit, and international monetary organizations. The committee has taken on a somewhat elevated profile in legislative debates since the financial crisis that sparked a deep and persistent economic recession in 2008.

★ BUDGET ★

The House Budget Committee, which has existed as a standing committee only since 1974 (unlike many House committees, the origins of which can be traced to the nineteenth century), has jurisdiction over legislation relating to the federal budget. Each year, it produces a budget resolution that serves as a blueprint for federal taxation and spending. Although the budget resolution does not have the force of law, it sets budgetary priorities that guide tax and spending legislation considered by the House.

★ HOMELAND SECURITY ★

The Homeland Security Committee was established in 2002 in the aftermath of the terrorist attacks of September 11, 2001. It has jurisdiction over Homeland Security Department programs, including those aimed at emergency response and preparedness, border security, and transportation security.

★ INTELLIGENCE ★

The Intelligence Committee has legislative jurisdiction over U.S. intelligence programs, and oversight authority over the government's intelligence agencies.

★ VETERANS AFFAIRS ★

The Veterans Affairs Committee has legislative and oversight authority over programs and operations carried out by the Department of Veterans Affairs. Such measures include veterans' rehabilitation programs, compensation and pensions, veterans' medical care, and national cemeteries.

★ TRANSPORTATION AND INFRASTRUCTURE ★

The Transportation and Infrastructure Committee deals with legislation relating to the construction and repair of bridges and public roads, mass transit, aviation, railroads, maritime transportation, and natural disaster preparedness. The committee has oversight authority over the Department of Transportation as well as the Army Corps of Engineers.

★ OVERSIGHT AND GOVERNMENT REFORM ★

The Oversight and Government Reform Committee is essentially an investigative body that has broad oversight authority over federal government departments, agencies, and programs. When a political scandal surfaces in Washington, D.C., this committee is highly likely to hold hearings and issue subpoenas. This is particularly true when one party controls the White House, and the other the House of Representatives. Recently, the committee, currently chaired by Rep. Darrell Issa (R-CA), subpoenaed former presidential candidate and current Secretary of State John Kerry to testify about the administration's handling of an attack on the U.S. embassy in Libya.[9]

★ ETHICS ★

The Ethics Committee, which is fairly young by standards of the House of Representatives (est. in 1967), carries out investigations of House members for alleged ethical misconduct. The committee is unique in that it is equally divided between Democrats and Republicans, and its work is carried out by a nonpartisan staff.

★ HOUSE ADMINISTRATION ★

The House Administration Committee has jurisdiction over legislation authorizing federal funds for House committees and daily operations, as well as security for the House side of the U.S. Capitol. It also has legislative and oversight responsibilities with regard to election law.

★ SCIENCE, SPACE, AND TECHNOLOGY ★

The Science, Space, and Technology Committee was established in the midst of the Cold War–era arms race between the United States and the Soviet Union. The committee has jurisdiction over energy program research and development, federal science and science education programs, and National Aeronautics and Space Administration (NASA) operations.

★ SMALL BUSINESS ★

The Small Business Committee has jurisdiction over programs and operations carried out by the Small Business Administration. It deals with legislation dealing with federal aid to and regulation of small businesses.

★ RULES COMMITTEE ★

Please see the previous chapter on the Rules Committee.

5: LEGISLATIVE SERVICE ORGANIZATIONS

L egislative service organizations (LSOs), most commonly referred to as caucuses (although they sometimes go by other labels), are coalitions of members devoted to a common legislative and/or political cause. These organizations have played a historically important role in the House of Representatives.

★ THE CONGRESSIONAL BLACK CAUCUS ★

The Congressional Black Caucus (CBC), a coalition of African American members of Congress, was comprised of 42 members of the House as of 2014.[1] While members of the U.S. Senate are also eligible for membership in the CBC, there have been very few African American senators since the organization's founding in 1971.[2] Prior to his election as president, then-Senator Barack Obama (D-IL) was a member of the CBC.[3] Until recently, there was only one African American senator: Tim Scott (R-SC), who in 2013 was appointed to fill the seat of Sen. Jim DeMint (R-SC), who had resigned to become president of the Heritage Foundation. Upon his appointment to the Senate, Scott declined to become a member of the CBC.[4] Cory Booker, however, a Democrat who in November 2013 won a special election to replace the late Sen. Frank Lautenberg (D-NJ), elected to join the caucus.[5] While the organization is technically nonpartisan, its political and policy objectives—which include fighting poverty, expanding access to health care, and removing barriers to voting—are much more closely aligned with the Democratic agenda than with Republican ideas.

Technically, the CBC does not officially require its members to be African American. This policy was tested following the 2006 midterm elections, in which Steve Cohen—a white Democrat who represents a congressional district that is 60 percent African American—sought to join the caucus. Cohen, a staunch liberal who has moved aggressively to demonstrate his commitment to the interests of his black constituents, had made a campaign promise to attempt to gain admission to the CBC. That pledge—and Cohen's ensuing efforts to make good on it—did not sit well with a number of African American House members. After a dispute between Cohen and the CBC that played out both in private and in the press, Rep. William Lacy Clay Jr.—the son of one of the CBC's founders, William Lacy Clay Sr.—released the following statement: "Quite simply, Rep. Cohen will have to accept what the rest of the country will have to accept—there has been an unofficial Congressional White Caucus for over 200 years, and now it's our turn to say who can join 'the club.' He does not, and cannot, meet the membership criteria, unless he can change his skin color. Primarily, we are concerned with the needs and concerns of the black population, and we will not allow white America to infringe on those objectives."[6]

Following the 2007 incident, however, Cohen worked to earn the trust and support of his colleagues in the CBC. He was rewarded in 2010 when, in his campaign to hold off a challenge in the Democratic primary from former Memphis Mayor Willie Herenton, Cohen received endorsements from CBC members.[7]

★ CONGRESSIONAL HISPANIC CAUCUS ★

Founded in 1976, the Congressional Hispanic Caucus is a coalition of Hispanic Democratic members of Congress. Although the group could once claim a bipartisan composition, Republicans formed the Congressional Hispanic Conference in 2003.[8] While the CHC is technically a nonpartisan organization, its legislative agenda reflects the center-left politics of its Democratic members, many of whom represent liberal urban congressional districts. The caucus also includes Senator Bob Menendez (D-NJ).[9]

★ THE BLUE DOG COALITION ★

The Blue Dogs are a coalition of moderate-to-conservative Democrats who have often opposed their leadership on matters pertaining to taxes and federal spending on social programs. Although the caucus was founded in 1995 after the Democrats lost control of Congress for the first time in forty years, the group's philosophy is rooted in the centrist politics of southern Democrats whose influence peaked in the 1990s during the Clinton administration. It should be noted, however, that Blue Dogs' political identity bears little resemblance to that of the southern Dixiecrats who dominated Democratic politics for much of the New Deal era.

Although many Blue Dogs opposed key components of President Obama's agenda, voters did not grant them a reprieve at the ballot box. Indeed, the Blue Dogs' numbers were decimated in the 2010 and 2012 elections, falling from 54 members in 2009 to 26 members in 2013.[10] A number of former Blue Dogs who hail from the South have left the coalition to join the Republican Party, including Ralph Hall of Texas, Billy Tauzin of Louisiana (who is now retired),[11] and Nathan Deal, who was elected governor of Georgia as a Republican in 2010.[12]

THE DEMOCRATIC STUDY GROUP: ★ A BRIEF HISTORY OF THE CAUCUS THAT ★ LIBERALIZED THE HOUSE

The Democratic Study Group (DSG) was a legislative service organization that played a critical role in a number of political struggles throughout much of the second half of the twentieth century, and yet remains largely unknown to the general public and has received scant attention from historians. The DSG, which became defunct in 1995, was a coalition of progressive House Democrats that challenged the dominant southern conservative wing of the Democratic Party. Indeed, to understand the historical significance of the DSG, one must first consider the political environment from which it arose.

When Rep. Eugene McCarthy convened an informal caucus of House liberals in 1957, the Democratic Party was less a political party than an illogical political coalition living on borrowed time. In the House and Senate, the southern, right-wing faction dominated the party's power structure. Although most Democratic voters and elected officials came from the moderate or liberal wings of the party, Congress' seniority system had allowed the Dixiecrats, long known for their longevity, to stifle the will of the party's majority. And despite the Democrats' enduring majorities in Congress during this era, the conservative coalition of Republicans and conservative Democrats would prove an insurmountable barrier to progressive reforms for decades.

Following the 1958 midterm elections, a handful of young House liberals decided to challenge the senior, entrenched southern Democratic machine. The progressive insurgency was the brainchild of Minnesota's Eugene McCarthy, Stewart Udall of Arizona, and Frank Thompson of New Jersey. Informally organized in 1957 as "McCarthy's Mavericks," and founded in earnest in 1959,[13] the DSG began a sophisticated, long-term effort to wrest control of the Democratic party from the southern conservatives who suffocated civil rights bills in their black holes of committees.

For the liberal insurgents, the Senate would always prove a less viable target for a progressive takeover; the chamber's rules leave the majority with little capacity to exert its will, allowing the conservative coalition to stonewall liberal legislative efforts for decades. But the

House was another matter. In the "people's house," the majority party had nearly free rein to impose its will on a minority faction that could do little more than resort to ineffectual protest. So if progressives could seize control of the party's structural power centers—the leadership posts and the chairmanships of committees—they could use the House's majoritarian rules to enable efforts to enact liberal legislation.

One critical victory for the DSG and its allies came just a few years after its founding, with the expansion of the House Rules Committee in 1961. While this landmark change to House rules may not sound like the kind of legislative victory that changes the course of history, one could argue that it did precisely that. This institutional reform was critical to passing civil rights legislation and the torrent of liberal legislation later signed into law by President Lyndon B. Johnson.

In January of 1961, liberals returned to Washington determined to break the iron grip with which the southern conservatives had ruled Congress for decades. On their side was a northern Democratic president, John F. Kennedy, whose administration had already begun to take steps to advance civil rights legislation even before the young Massachusetts senator assumed the oval office.

Speaker Sam Rayburn, despite representing a white, conservative congressional district in Texas, personally supported civil rights legislation.[14] At the time, it was clear that progress on such bills would be impossible without making major changes to the Rules Committee, which as explained in an earlier chapter has the ultimate say over which legislation is voted on and ultimately passed by the House. Whereas nowadays the Rules Committee is controlled by allies of the majority party's leadership in the House, this was not the case during the New Deal and civil rights eras. In 1961, the Rules Committee was chaired by Rep. Howard Smith of Virginia, a right-wing Democrat with a long history of hostility to racial equality. Smith, along with his ally, Rep. William Colmer (D-MS), had successfully formed a coalition with the Rules Committee's conservative Republican members to block the legislative priorities of the party's liberal wing and leadership.[15]

Any effort to reform the Rules Committee seemingly involved taking steps to purge conservative Democrats from the panel, and such a plan was indeed considered by the Democratic leadership. Yet Speaker Rayburn, who had a well-earned reputation for fairness and commanded loyalties in both parties, ultimately opted for a tactic intended to allow Smith and Colmer to save face. Rather than expel Colmer, the Speaker backed a plan to add two liberals to the committee, thereby handing a one-vote majority to the liberal coalition. Rayburn described the plan as "the way to embarrass nobody if they didn't want to be embarrassed."[16]

The enlargement of the Rules Committee marked

a historic shift not only for the House, but for the Democratic Party. Indeed, with this critical victory by liberals over the previously dominant Dixiecrats, the Democratic Party had finally begun to heed Hubert Humphrey's call in 1948 to "get out of the shadow of states rights and march forthrightly into the bright sunshine of human rights."[17]

Yet efforts to win top leadership spots would prove elusive for decades. Rep. John McCormack (D-MA), who succeeded Rayburn as Speaker in 1962, had a decidedly good rapport with the party's southern faction. Rep. Mo Udall, a liberal champion and key DSG member, would suffer an embarrassing defeat in his campaign to oust McCormack of Massachusetts as Speaker of the House in 1969.[18] When Udall then ran for Majority Leader the following year, he was again soundly defeated, this time by Louisiana Congressman Hale Boggs. Udall, who was arguably one of the most quotable politicians in American history, is on record as having said that the experiences had taught him the difference between a cactus and a caucus: "With a cactus, the pricks are on the outside."[19] Ultimately, it was not until 1981, when one-time DSG chairman Tom Foley rose to become the Democratic Whip (eventually going on to become Speaker),[20] that a major DSG figure assumed a top leadership position within the Democratic caucus.

Despite being founded by "good-government" liberals, the DSG was not immune to ethical missteps or political scandals. One of its founding members would be swept from office in 1980 after becoming embroiled in the firestorm surrounding the Abscam scandal.[21] (Abscam refers to the sting operation carried out by the FBI that recorded members of Congress accepting bribes. The scandal was dramatized in the Oscar-nominated film *American Hustle*.) Still, the DSG's reformist mission undoubtedly attracted a membership with a sincere interest in ethical and transparent governance, a cause that drew the ire of other members of the Democratic caucus. Barely one decade after Abscam, New York Democrat and former DSG Chair Matthew McHugh—whom Rep. David Obey (D-WI), a DSG member who served more than four decades in the House, described as "what every Catholic mother wants her son to grow up to be"[22]—would be called upon by then-Speaker Foley to lead an investigation of the 1992 House banking scandal, which had ensnared several of his fellow Democrats.

Despite the unusual talent that constituted the DSG, the group was, like any political faction, subject to the electoral waves brought about by dramatic changes in public opinion. The group seemed to be clearly ascendant following the midterm elections of 1974, when the Watergate scandal swelled the ranks of DSG membership. And in 1975, the DSG would prove to be more than a regional faction of liberals confined to the North and the Midwest. The group that was founded with a decidedly anti-southern outlook would elect Rep. Bob Eckhardt, a Houston Democrat who took liberal stances on civil rights, as its first southern chairman.[23]

Yet 1980 would also prove to be a seminal year, as the "Reagan Revolution" reinvigorated the conservative coalition and the party's conservative wing. President Jimmy Carter lost his reelection bid in a landslide to ex–California governor Ronald Reagan. Democrats suffered major losses nationally, and liberal legends went down to defeat at every level of government. Senators Birch Bayh of Indiana, Frank Church of Idaho, Gaylord Nelson of Wisconsin, and George McGovern of South Dakota—the Democratic nominee for president in 1972—lost their reelection bids.[24] In the House, Democrats lost 35 seats, as southerners, who had already begun to cast their votes for Republican presidential candidates, threw their support to Republicans running in down-ballot races. Eckhardt, who had endured in his culturally conservative Houston-based district for seven terms, would lose his seat.[25] Tom Foley struggled to hold onto his seat, winning with just 52 percent of the vote.[26]

By the early 1990s, the one-time agitators had effectively won their battle—at least with regard to the DSG's original purpose. The giants of the party's conservative wing had vanished—had either retired, been defeated for reelection, or switched parties. And the Democratic leadership and committee chairmen were now unequivocal partisans of the progressive faction. With Foley now wielding the Speaker's gavel, Rep. David R. Obey would soon seize the reins of the Appropriations Committee, defeating the more senior and decidedly less activist Neal Smith (D-IA).[27] Martin Sabo of Minnesota now chaired the Budget Committee, after California Rep. Leon Panetta left the House to join the Clinton administration.[28]

Yet in a matter of months the group would be abruptly disbanded. The Democratic collapse and GOP revolution of 1994 would leave the party's membership in Congress in the political wilderness for more than a decade. And although the Democrats would regain their majorities in the 2006 elections, the DSG would never be revived.

On December 7, 1994, the Democratic Study Group issued a "special report," entitled, "DSG Eliminated?" A month after the Republicans had won control of the House of Representatives for the first time in forty years, the Republican Conference had voted to advise the House Oversight Committee to eliminate the Democratic Study Group.

The decision, of course, was hardly surprising. In its thirty-five years, the DSG had grown from a caucus of liberal reformers and agitators to a membership that included virtually every Democrat in the body. The group's legislative research service had evolved into the most influential and trusted source for information on bills that came before the House—so trusted, that some Republicans now subscribed to the service.

Indeed, the DSG had no equal in Congress when it came to the flow of information on legislation. A survey conducted by the House Commission on Legislative Review indicated that 75 percent of House Democrats and their staff regarded DSG as the most important source of such information.

The DSG, faced with the prospect of disbandment, published a seven-page report to plead its case. It detailed its thirty-five-year history, its core mission, its legislative achievements, and even pointed to its Republican subscribers as proof that its legislative service was indispensable. It contended that the group was not a lobbying organization, but merely briefed members on legislation headed for the House floor. This was an accurate, if incomplete, argument. To be sure, the DSG was no lobbying outfit. Its staff had no lobbyists. Rather, paid staff consisted mainly of analysts, who wrote reports on legislation, and their editors.

Yet neither the DSG's mission, nor its history, could be described as a briefing service. The DSG did take positions on major issues and legislation, and its elected membership in the House spearheaded some of the most critical institutional reforms the House had ever undertaken. Some of those changes may have changed the course of history, particularly on civil rights.

DSG weekly legislative reports were nonpartisan briefings: they summarized the legislation, offered information on the administration's views, and provided background information on the issue that the bill dealt with. But their "special reports" were, indeed, position papers. They took stances on some of the most controversial issues before the Congress. From the group's inception, its mission was to organize a faction of the Democratic Party to advocate for progressive stances on civil rights, the Vietnam War, and economic policy. And although by 1994 the Vietnam War was long over and civil rights legislation had become the law of the land, the group indisputably retained its left-leaning, reformist orientation.

That some Republicans were willing to pay a total of $4,000 for the DSG's legislative information services was likely of little comfort to the newly empowered GOP leadership. For a short time, DSG provided its services to members as a private entity, before becoming truly defunct. The nonpartisan Congressional Quarterly then purchased the group's legislative services, stripping them of any ideological affiliation. And thus, after more than thirty years as the driving force behind the liberal wing of the House Democratic caucus, the Democratic Study Group met its abrupt end.

☆ 6: FLOOR DEBATE ☆

Portrayals of the House of Representatives in popular culture may have left the impression that, as the House considers legislation, representatives gather to listen, persuade, and even perhaps be persuaded on the most important matters facing the country—that, against the backdrop of a packed House chamber, spirited debates ensue, and members sit and listen attentively while remaining open to casting a vote in either direction. Such an impression would be inaccurate. With notable exceptions, floor debate in the House is often uneventful, unsurprising, heavily scripted, and sparsely attended. ("Floor debate" literally refers to debate on legislation that occurs on the House floor.) At any given moment, only a handful of members may be present in an otherwise empty House chamber. When the House tackles legislation that is highly controversial, and for which the outcome of its passage is in doubt, debate can certainly be lively, and even riveting at times. Much of the House's work, however, deals with legislation that is so noncontroversial that the public never even learns that it was voted on. Such items include resolutions praising historical figures and measures that rename post offices.

Other bills may be more consequential, but unlikely to attract much opposition, and are generally brought up for debate under suspension of the rules, a process described earlier. One such example of a noncontroversial bill scheduled for consideration under suspension of the rules during the 113th Congress (which lasted from January 3, 2013, to January 3, 2015) was HR (which stands for House of Representatives) 4801 (every bill has its own number), introduced by Rep. Adam Kinzinger (R-IL), a measure that simply directs the Secretary of Energy to issue a report assessing the impact of thermal insulation on both energy and water use for potable hot water.[1]

The "floor manager" for a bill is generally the chairman of the committee from which that bill originated. For example, the floor manager for a bill relating to education policy would typically be the chairman of the Education and the Workforce Committee. If a bill has gone through multiple committees before being brought to the House floor, the chairmen of those committees may share floor management duties.

The floor manager does exactly what his or her name implies: coordinate floor debate on the bill being debated. He or she generally does so in consultation with the ranking member of the committee from the minority party, although the extent of this consultation depends on the degree of partisan tension present during the debate and the relationship between the chairman and the ranking member. The floor manager and his or her minority party counterpart field requests from members to speak on the bill, and determine how much time each member will be allocated during the debate.

If the rule (the resolution reported by the Rules Committee) accompanying a bill allows for amendments, the House debates those amendments as the "Committee of the Whole." This confusingly termed legislative device simply refers to the entire membership of the House as a committee. For example, if the House debates a bill for which the Rules Committee has allowed four amendments, it would first proceed with a period of "general debate" on the underlying bill. Then, the House would "resolve itself" into the Committee of the Whole for the consideration of the four amendments. Once those amendments have been voted on, the Committee "rises" and the House (no longer the Committee of the Whole) then votes on final passage of the underlying bill.

Although debate can be heated, the chamber's rules do demand a certain degree of decorum. As noted earlier when describing Speaker Tip O'Neill's confrontation with a young Newt Gingrich on the House floor, a member can lose his or her speaking rights for the duration of the day if that member's remarks are deemed overly personal. Demands that another member's words be "taken down" are fairly common, but the offending member usually asks unanimous consent from the House to withdraw his or her words, and thereby retains full speaking rights and does not bring House proceedings to a screeching halt. During debate on a bill that repealed health insurance companies' exemptions from antitrust laws, former Rep. Anthony Weiner (D-NY), who (prior to his professional unraveling due to a sex scandal) was known for his feisty and caustic debating style, declared: "The Republican Party is the wholly owned subsidiary of the insurance industry." Rep. Dan Lungren (R-CA) asked that Weiner's words be taken down. A short time late, Weiner asked to withdraw those words, and then offered a revised version: "Make no mistake about it, every single Republican I have ever met in my entire life is a wholly owned subsidiary of the insurance industry!" Lungren again demanded that Weiner's words be taken down.

Finally, Weiner again withdrew his remarks—this time without attempting to reiterate the same sentiment.[2] The House then proceeded with its business, and passed the bill overwhelmingly.

In one of the most startlingly personal and ugly attacks ever launched by one House member against another—and toward a member of his own party—Rep. Bob Dornan (R-CA), a conservative firebrand with a penchant for theatrics and the demeanor of a schoolyard bully, outed Rep. Steve Gunderson (R-WI) as gay during a debate on the House floor. During debate on an amendment that would have prohibited school districts from portraying gays and lesbians in a positive light, Dornan said of Gunderson: "My fellow Republican has a revolving door in his closet. He's out, he's in. He's out, he's in. Now I guess you're out because you spoke at a huge homosexual dinner." Those remarks stunned Dornan's colleagues, and were clearly out of order. Dornan then received unanimous consent to withdraw his words, and debate continued.[3]

At times, floor debate can become deeply personal. As the House votes on legislation relating to issues that have personally affected its members in powerful ways, their speeches depart from the usual debate. One such instance occurred in 2007, when the Democratic-controlled House had taken up the Employment Non-Discrimination Act (ENDA), a bill that prohibited employers from discriminating against people because of their sexual orientation. Shortly before a vote on final passage, the Republican minority offered a "motion to recommit with instructions" the ENDA bill that would have sent it back to the committee that reported it. While the Democratic leadership likely could have mustered the votes required to beat back a motion to simply send the bill back to the committee, this motion had instructions to amend the bill so as to define marriage as an institution between a man and a woman. Thus, a vote against the Republican motion to derail the bill could have been portrayed (in political ads) as a vote in favor of legalizing same-sex marriage.

To those who are just beginning to tune in to the political debate, the notion that supporting the right of same-sex couples to marry—which is increasingly viewed as a fundamental human right—might seem strange, or even downright ludicrous. But the political climate with respect to marriage equality was radically different in 2007 than it was during the second term of the Obama administration, when the federal courts began striking down same-sex marriage bans at a breakneck pace. None of the major Democratic candidates for president in 2008 (Barack Obama, Hillary Clinton, or John Edwards) supported legalizing same-sex marriage. Sen. John Kerry (D-MA) did not embrace marriage equality as the Democratic nominee for president in 2004. Thus, in 2007, supporting marriage rights for gay and lesbian couples was still seen as a political liability for Democrats representing politically competitive regions of the country.

It is within the context described above that Rep. Barney Frank (D-MA), a liberal Democrat who was the first openly gay member of the House of Representatives, made an extraordinarily personal speech in leading the opposition to the GOP motion to derail the ENDA bill. While he had built a reputation as one of the House's most skilled debaters, known for his quick wit and aggressive style, Frank was not among the House's most sentimental or emotional members. Yet on this day, he invoked his own experiences facing discrimination as a gay man, and spoke of his sense of responsibility to give voice to the gay and lesbian individuals who, not enjoying positions of power, continued to face discrimination at school and at the workplace. Frank, his voice at times shaking with emotion, made the following plea to his colleagues:

Mr. Speaker, we say here that we don't take things personally, and usually that's true. Members, Mr. Speaker, will have to forgive me—I take it a little personally. . . . As we sit here today there are millions of Americans in states where this [the ENDA bill] is not the law. . . . I used to be someone subject to this prejudice. And through luck, circumstance, I got to be a big shot. I'm

now above that prejudice. But I feel an obligation to 15 year olds dreading to go to school
because of the torments, to people afraid they'll
lose their job in a gas station if someone finds
out who they love. I feel an obligation to use the
status I have been lucky enough to get to help
them. And I want to ask my colleagues here,
Mr. Speaker, on a personal basis, please don't fall
for this sham. Don't send me out of here having
failed to help those people.[4]

Floor debate in the House of Representatives differs considerably from the discourse that one observes
in the U.S. Senate. While senators routinely give long
(critics might say bloviating) speeches, House debate
tends to be more focused and regimented, with members being allotted limited time for their remarks. (At
the end of the day—when legislative business has concluded, and there are no more bills to consider—House
members may give what are known as "special orders"
speeches. Unlike speeches during floor debate on
legislation, these can indeed be quite lengthy. Generally,
the press gallery has emptied out by this hour, and
few are present to observe members' remarks.) Remarks
tend to be more partisan, fiery, and to the point than
senators' speeches.

The following debate, intended to serve as an example of typical floor debate, concerned a rule providing

for consideration of a Republican-sponsored budget resolution. It is, in many ways, typical of debate in the House. Participants included Rep. Adam Putnam (R-FL), a rising star in the Republican Party who has since left the House to run for state-wide office; Rep. Louise Slaughter, then (and now) the ranking Democrat on the Rules Committee; Rep. David Obey (D-WI), a veteran liberal member and highly skilled debater; and Rep. Jeb Hensarling (R-TX), an articulate and politically talented emerging leader of House conservatives. During the debate, Slaughter lit into her political opponents over their budgetary priorities:

> Mr. Speaker, every justification of the budget we have heard today presents it as a noble and responsible attempt to respond to the harsh economic realities facing our nation and our people. But when we examine it objectively, we can't avoid seeing the reality behind the pretense. The bill is designed to do everything it can to protect the record tax cuts for the richest of Americans. For the [Republican] majority, that is more important than educating our children or providing health care to the veterans or helping Americans raise themselves out of poverty, or even protecting our country from the consequences of either national disasters or mounting national debt.

The authors and supporters of the legislation will tell us that if we wish to avoid increasing our national deficit, which they have already driven to unprecedented heights, we have no choice but to spend on the programs that Americans rely on the most while they are busily cutting out the revenues that come into the government. . . . Republicans who promised to leave no child behind will be cutting education funding by $45.3 billion, and the budget of the Department of Education by $2.2 billion. Now, not content to make education less rewarding in the present, they apparently want to make our students worry more about loan payments in the future. The bill eliminates all mandatory spending on student loans, leaving congressional appropriators to somehow find $600 million to meet the students' needs.

Putnam, leading floor debate for the Republican side, responded to Slaughter's critique of his party's budgetary blueprint:

Mr. Speaker, the gentlewoman raised the issue of education funding. I would point out that the facts are a bit counter to her assertion. Take special education, something that has long been a priority of both [Republican and Democratic] sides of the aisle. Special education funding goes up for the sixth consecutive year, an increase of $100 million this year, which is an estimated $1,500 per student, reaching almost 7 million students who have special needs.

On Pell Grants, the budget provides $12.7 billion in available Pell Grant aid, for an average grant of nearly $2,500. More than 5.2 million students would be eligible for these grants, an increase of sixty thousand students over the previous year.

Title I, those schools that serve the most in need, the resolution provides nearly $13 billion for title I grants to help schools in the high poverty communities move ahead with No Child Left Behind [an education program championed by President George W. Bush]; $1 billion for the Reading First program, and increased funding for charter schools, magnet schools, voluntary public school choice, all substantial funding for these very important programs.

Obey, who was one of a handful of members on both sides of the aisle who could debate effectively while speaking extemporaneously, was incredulous:

Mr. Speaker, for weeks we have been wondering whether the Republican moderates were going to stick to their guns when they said they knew that it was wrong to pass a budget that provided $40 billion in tax cuts for people making $1 million a year while you are squeezing the guts out of education and health programs. We now know the answer. They are doing a poor imitation of Bert Lahr, the Cowardly Lion in "The Wizard of Oz." I wish Bert were here. He would cry at their performance.

The fact is they are now selling out for a promise that if sometime in the deep, dark, distant future somebody does something to change this budget resolution, then there might be a table scrap or two left for additional education and health care. There is about as much chance of that happening as there is of the Chicago Cubs winning the pennant this year.

With respect to what the gentleman from Florida said on education, the fact is the Congress promised the states that on special education we would pay for 40 percent of the costs. Each year for the last 3 years, the federal share of the cost of special education has been cut by budgets that you have voted for.

You talk about Pell Grants. The fact is it costs $3,400 more to go to a 4-year public college today than it did 5 years ago. The President wanted to solve that by adding $100 to the Pell

Grant program. House Republicans said, no, that was too much. You cut it to $50, and then when you sent it to the Senate, you cut out the rest of the 50 bucks.

So, in 5 years you have not done one whit to make it easier for people to go to college by increasing the Pell Grants.

So do not give us your crocodile tears, and do not brag incidentally about how much you have increased education for the last 6 years, because there are $16 billion in the education budget today that would not be there if we had not dragged you kicking and screaming into supporting Labor-Health budgets that in the end were higher than the original House Republican budget.

So I do not mind if the gentleman wants to live in the Land of Oz. Just do not take us there with you.

Representative Hensarling spoke next from the Republican side:

I am reminded yet again that people are entitled to their own opinions, but they are not entitled to their own facts, and, Mr. Speaker, maybe we ought to get a few of the facts on the table. Let us just take a look in our rearview mirror over the last 10 years and see how much money the Federal Government has been spending.

International affairs is up 89.1 percent; natural resources and environment, 43.8 percent; commerce and housing credit, 28.4. Since we have been discussing education training and employment, in 10 years that budget has gone from $53 billion to $114 billion. That is an increase of 113 percent. I mean, Mr. Speaker, how much do we need here in Federal spending? Should it be a 130 percent increase in 10 years, 150, 200? We have to remember, also, Mr. Speaker, where is this money coming from? Although maybe there is literally a printing press down the road, figuratively there is not one. All of this money is coming from some American family, and every time we are increasing some Federal program, we are taking it away from some family program. Right now, again, budgets are about values, and they are about dollars and cents, and ultimately, this debate does come down again to taxes and spending.

The Democrats have said that we are offering all these great tax cuts. I looked very closely in the budget. I am having a little trouble finding that. What I do find is that we are going to prevent a huge automatic tax increase engineered by the other side. It is very fascinating to me in the Federal city how spending is forever; yet tax relief seems to be temporary.[5]

★ THE PREVIOUS QUESTION MOTION ★

The majority party in the House has at its disposal a potent weapon that enables it to end floor debate and force an up-or-down vote. This maneuver is known as the "previous question motion." When a member declares: "I move the previous question," the House majority has invoked the privilege provided by the chamber's rules to exert control over floor debate. This motion, in conjunction with the power of the Rules Committee (as explained in an earlier chapter), is largely responsible for the House's majoritarian character.

The U.S. Senate has no such motion, which makes it far more difficult for the majority party in that chamber to end debate on legislation. The absence of the previous question motion in the Senate explains why the legislative process in that chamber seems to move at a glacial pace. Yet the Senate brought this predicament on itself. In 1805, Vice President Aaron Burr—who was preparing to leave public life after killing former Treasury Secretary Alexander Hamilton in a duel—proposed revisions to the Senate's rules. In so doing, he recommended that the upper chamber eliminate the previous question motion, which he regarded as redundant. Senators took his advice, and quite accidentally created the filibuster.[6]

7: CASE STUDY — ☆ THE AFFORDABLE ☆ CARE ACT

On the evening of March 21, 2010, Rep. David R. Obey of Wisconsin, a man who had served nearly half a century in public office and who was first elected to the House of Representatives in 1969, rose to preside over the House chamber. The hour was late, and the House was preparing for a momentous vote on what was arguably one of the most important yet controversial bills of the last forty years. Within minutes, House members would decide the fate of a health-care reform bill that was the centerpiece of President Obama's domestic agenda, and that its supporters believed would be a landmark law that advanced the cause of justice in America.

To the bill's opponents, the stakes could hardly have

been higher. The fight over comprehensive health-care reform had been brutal and seemingly never-ending. Republicans in Congress mounted a spirited and unified attack against the bill that, on more than one occasion, appeared on the verge of defeating it permanently. Many congressional Democrats—and some advisors in President Obama's inner circle—were urging that the administration and its allies abandon its efforts, fearing a catastrophic legislative failure from which the new president would never recover.

Moreover, the Democrats lacked the united front with which Republicans opposed the Affordable Care Act. Indeed, the bill threatened to splinter the Democratic coalition that had come to power with huge majorities following the 2008 election. The "Blue Dog" Democrats—a coalition of conservative Democrats that was frequently at odds with the party's more progressive leadership—had serious reservations about passing a major health-care overhaul. In a separate but not entirely unrelated conflict, a coalition of socially conservative Democrats who opposed abortion rights threatened to scuttle the bill unless concessions were made regarding insurance coverage for abortion services.

On March 21, 2010, when Obey brought the vote to a close and declared that the legislation had passed, the House of Representatives had indeed made history. For more than sixty years, presidents had tried and failed to enact comprehensive health-care reform at the federal level. Yet the legislative history of the Affordable Care Act can be traced to the weeks leading up to President Obama's inauguration on a frigid winter day in 2009. The story of the health-care reform effort in many ways began in the hospital room of an ailing elder statesman of the Democratic Party—one who would not live to see its enactment. The following case study is intended to illuminate the legislative process that culminated in the enactment of the historic health-care law, the merits of which continue to be contentiously debated as of this writing. Out of necessity, the case study details legislative maneuverings concerning the Senate's consideration of the bill. Given that this book is devoted to enhancing the layman's understanding of the House of Representatives, however, it is admittedly written from a House-centric perspective.

★ PROLOGUE: LAYING THE GROUND WORK ★

In October of 2008, then-Sen. Barack Obama of Illinois appeared poised for a historic victory in the presidential election over Sen. John McCain (R-AZ). Democrats, already in control of the House and Senate following a Democratic wave in the 2006 midterm elections, appeared highly likely to increase their majorities in both chambers. For Sen. Edward M.

"Ted" Kennedy, the prospect of Obama's election signaled his last and best hope to help craft legislation providing for the enactment of universal health-care coverage, which Kennedy called "the cause of my life." Kennedy, after all, had been an early and critical supporter of Obama during the presidential primaries, and the young Illinois senator was often compared to Kennedy's late brother, President John F. Kennedy. Having seen the Clinton administration's health-care reform effort collapse in 1993, Kennedy had hoped to move quickly. Even before Obama's election, Kennedy conducted meetings with lobbyists and members of both parties from his hospital bed.[1] As chairman of the powerful Health, Education, Labor and Pensions (HELP) Committee in the Senate, Kennedy was in a position to exert considerable influence over health-care reform legislation.

Despite his efforts, Kennedy's declining health sidelined him during the debate for which he had waited his entire political life. Moreover, the absence of the "liberal lion" (as he was known) created a political void in the Senate—a void which would be filled by Sen. Max Baucus (D-MT), a far more conservative Democrat whose commitment to health-care reform seemed difficult to gauge. In a clear demonstration of his intention to assert his political clout during the Senate's consideration of health reform, Baucus published a "white paper"[2] laying out a blueprint for health-care reform just eight days after Obama's election as president. Baucus's plan mirrored much of what Obama had called for in campaigning on universal health care, as it:

1. created an exchange in which plans would compete with one another, and through which the uninsured would receive subsidies to purchase insurance;
2. expanded existing government health insurance programs to further reduce the number of uninsured; and
3. overhauled the health insurance market by instituting new regulations (such as prohibiting insurers from denying coverage to those with pre-existing medical conditions).

Much of the media's attention in the early days of the health-care reform effort focused on Baucus's intentions and on the U.S. Senate generally. This is no surprise, as senators—who represent entire states—receive more press coverage than House members. Yet in retrospect, it seems clear that Baucus's outsized influence over the process of crafting health-care legislation put the Democratic Party's liberal wing at a disadvantage. Baucus had flatly rejected a single-payer approach (the health-care system favored by many European countries), and did not insist on a new government-run insurance plan that would compete with private insurers. While single-payer was seen as a pipe dream from the very beginning, the government-run plan—known as the "public option"—was seen by progressives as not only achievable, but a critical element of meaningful reform.

NAVIGATING HEALTH-CARE REFORM THROUGH COMMITTEES

In the House, the chairmen of the three committees with legislative jurisdiction over the bill joined together in an effort to avoid the intraparty splintering that had brought down legislative efforts in the past, including President Clinton's health-care initiative in 1993. Those chairmen were:

- Rep. George Miller (D-CA), the chairman of the Education and Labor Committee, a tough-minded liberal who was first elected to the House in 1974, and was a close ally of then-Speaker Nancy Pelosi;
- Rep. Henry Waxman (D-CA), the chairman of the Energy and Commerce Committee, another liberal veteran of the House; and
- Rep. Charlie Rangel (D-NY), the chairman of the Ways and Means Committee, who has

represented a Harlem-based congressional district since 1970.

In March, April, and May of 2009, the three committees held hearings on health reform, and witnesses called by both parties testified. In June, the committee chairmen described above, with the blessing of House Speaker Pelosi, released a working draft of their bill.[3] It required all Americans to obtain health insurance, created a health insurance exchange where plans could be purchased, expanded Medicaid (the health insurance plan for the poor) to cover more of the working poor, required larger employers to provide insurance to their employees or pay a fine and, reflecting the liberal dispositions of the three chairmen as well as liberal strength in the House Democratic caucus, included a public option.

On July 14, the House's first legislative attempt since the early nineties at universal health care was formally introduced as HR 3200, entitled America's Affordable Health Choices Act of 2009. The bill, which included a number of new provisions—most significantly a new tax on the wealthiest Americans to pay for the expansion of health coverage—was then referred to the three committees mentioned above for their consideration. During committee markups of the bill, Republican members offered amendments to gut the underlying legislation, all of which were defeated. Efforts to restrict coverage for abortions, while also defeated, were the first warning signs that Democratic supporters of the bill would face resistance from a group of Democrats who opposed abortion rights and threatened to derail the bill if their concerns were not addressed.[4]

During the committees' consideration of HR 3200, Republicans were outnumbered by their Democratic counterparts in the majority, and were unsuccessful in their attempts to alter the bill. Moreover, Democratic supporters of health-care reform viewed Republican efforts to amend the bill as part of a strategy to kill (rather than improve) the underlying legislation. Democrats, skeptical if not incredulous about Republicans' claims to be acting in good faith, saw no rationale for negotiating with the minority in the hopes of achieving a bipartisan deal. (A very different process played out in the Senate, where Baucus led negotiations among a group of senators from both parties. Those negotiations, it should be noted, did not prove fruitful, as will be discussed shortly.)

The liberal Democratic membership on the Ways and Means and Education and Labor Committees managed to keep the bill relatively intact during their markups. During the Energy and Commerce Committee's markup of HR 3200, however, the Democrats encountered resistance from a moderate-to-conservative bloc known as the "Blue Dog Coalition."[5] By threatening to align with Republican members of the committee to form a coalition capable of defeating the bill, the Blue Dogs had enormous leverage in their negotiations with Democratic leaders. House liberals, who did not want to see their party's signature domestic policy initiative watered down, were furious. Negotiations between the Blue Dogs, led by then-Rep. Mike Ross (D-AR) (who retired in 2012), and Chairman Henry Waxman (D-CA) grew increasingly heated. Bristling at their demands, Waxman at one point threatened to abandon the committee's consideration of the bill, and urge Democratic leaders to bring the bill directly to the House floor for a vote and bypass his committee entirely. "We're not going to let them empower Republicans to control the committee," Waxman declared.[6]

Despite Waxman's rhetoric, circumventing Blue Dog opposition to the bill on the Energy and Commerce Committee by bringing the bill directly to the House floor was likely never a viable option. The Blue Dog Coalition claimed a membership of 52 House Democrats in 2009,[7] and such a brazen move to undermine their influence would likely have cost the Democrats the votes they needed to pass the bill. Thus, negotiations continued, and in the end, the Blue Dogs did in fact win major concessions. While the public option survived, it was significantly watered down. Rather than creating a public insurance plan that used Medicare's pricing system—as the bill initially called for in order to drive down insurance costs—the public option envisioned in the bill reported by the Energy and Commerce Committee forced the new program to negotiate prices with medical providers.[8] This change would have made it difficult for the new insurance program to fulfill the function envisioned by its proponents—that through the mechanism of market competition, it would result in lower health costs for consumers of private plans.

While the weakening of the public option was the most substantial policy concession made by party leaders, the Blue Dogs won another victory in their negotiations that, arguably, was devastating to the prospects of passing health-care reform in the House. Specifically, Democratic leaders had acquiesced to Blue Dog demands that the House delay voting on a health bill at least until September. Such a delay, the Blue Dogs contended, would give members time to gauge the mood of the public with respect to a comprehensive health-care overhaul.[9] Thus, the Energy and Commerce Committee concluded its consideration of HR 3200 on July 31, in time for the House to adjourn for its traditional August recess, in which members typically fulfill duties in their districts. As Democratic members returned home to greet their constituents, they were woefully unprepared for the onslaught of attacks launched against the health-care reform effort at town hall meetings. In competitive districts—those in which

Democrats would be vulnerable to challenges by GOP opponents—angry constituents showed up to voice their displeasure, outrage, and disgust at the legislative process that was unfolding in Washington. Moreover, they expressed disdain, scorn, and in many cases unbridled hatred toward the still-recently elected President Obama.

At town hall meetings that would become infamous, members were heckled, shouted down, and drowned out by their constituents. At times, rage appeared about to boil over. At a meeting in Tampa held by Rep. Kathy Castor (D-FL), police arrived to calm a crowd that had grown disorderly and even violent as a fistfight broke out between constituents on opposing sides of the health-care debate.[10] In Maryland, an activist burned an effigy of Rep. Frank Kravotil, a Democrat who represented a Republican-leaning district.[11]

While members were generally restrained in their responses, some saw no reason to handle those who vote to reelect or defeat them with kid gloves. After one town hall attendee told Rep. Pete Stark (D-CA), "Don't pee on my leg and tell me it's raining," to which Stark responded: "I wouldn't dignify you by peeing on your leg. It wouldn't be worth wasting the urine."[12]

In the midst of the chaos of the summer of 2009, Senator Kennedy succumbed to brain cancer. He died on August 25. Given the heavily Democratic nature of Massachusetts's electorate, it seemed assured that a supporter of health reform would replace the Senate's Liberal Lion. A special election to replace Kennedy was scheduled for January 19, 2010, and the state's Democratic governor, Deval Patrick, appointed a former Kennedy staffer to serve as an interim senator until the newly elected senator could be sworn in.[13]

If the goal of delaying a vote on health-care reform legislation was to generate support for it in the electorate, all did not go remotely according to plan. A CNN poll released on September 2, 2009 found a bare majority of Americans (51 percent) now opposed the reform effort moving through Congress,[14] which represented a slight (although statistically insignificant) erosion in support from earlier in the summer, when a bare majority had supported an effort. Moreover, vulnerable Democrats could not ignore what they had seen and experienced in their districts. There could be no mistake: the Democratic push to overhaul the nation's health-care system was fraught with peril, particularly for those who had to run for reelection in competitive and Republican-leaning districts.

Recognizing that the cornerstone of his domestic policy agenda was in serious jeopardy, President Obama addressed a joint session of Congress on September 9, 2009. In his address, he called for action and vowed to keep an open mind to Republican suggestions to improve the bill. He sharply rebuked, however, critics who had deliberately misrepresented the bill, as some had indisputably done. Opponents had raised the specter of so-called "death panels" in which the proposed health-care law would supposedly euthanize the old and the vulnerable. Sen. Chuck Grassley (R-IA), a key figure in the health-care reform negotiations in the Senate, told a crowd that they were right to fear a "government program that determines if you're going to pull the plug on grandma."[15] In his speech, Obama took aim at these attacks, excoriating the death-panel claim as "a lie, plain and simple."[16] Obama also reiterated that the bill would not provide coverage to undocumented immigrants, at which point Rep. Joe Wilson (R-SC), in an unprece-dented display of hostility and disrespect during a presidential address, shouted "You lie!" After refusing to apologize publicly on the House floor, Wilson was formally admonished by the House for his actions by a vote of 240–179.[17]

★ THE HOUSE PASSES ITS HEALTH-CARE REFORM BILL ★

On October 29, a reconciled version of the legislation that passed the three House committees was finally introduced, this time as HR 3962, the Affordable Health Care for America Act. This bill contained the weakened public option negotiated between the

Democratic leadership and the Blue Dogs, as well as a 5.4 percent surtax on Americans earning more than $1 million per year. On November 7, the House passed the "rule" providing for debate on the bill. In addition to providing for debate time, the rule allowed for two amendments to be considered—one by Rep. Bart Stupak (D-MI), that would have prohibited federal funding for health plans that covered abortion, and a second amendment that served as the Republicans' "alternative" health bill, and contained a number of their proposals.[18]

Sixty-four Democrats joined 176 Republicans to pass the Stupak amendment that restricted funding for abortion coverage.[19] Despite their victory, pro-choice Democrats still hoped that Stupak's language would be negotiated out of the bill in the Senate, or in negotiations between the two chambers. At 11:15 p.m. on November 7, the House passed its comprehensive health-care reform bill by a narrow vote of 220–215. Democratic leaders were jubilant, and understandably so. The vote was historic, and marked a turning point in the fight for universal health care in the United States. Yet there were clear signs of danger for the Democratic majority. Thirty-nine Democrats had abandoned their party, nearly all of them vulnerable members who faced an uphill battle for reelection.[20] And health-care reform's fate in the Senate was far from assured.

★ THE SENATE PASSES ITS HEALTH BILL ★

Indeed, even as proponents of health-care reform hoped that its passage in the House portended momentum, they watched proceedings in the Senate with increasing concern. While the Senate HELP Committee had reported the bill on July 15, the Senate Finance Committee, which was made up of a more conservative membership (and led by the more conservative Chairman Max Baucus [D-MT]), appeared to be stalled in its efforts to produce a bill.

Adamant that health-care reform legislation needed to be bipartisan in order to be lasting, Baucus led negotiations among the "Gang of Six," a group made up of three Democrats and three Republicans. The three Democrats were Baucus, Sen. Kent Conrad (D-ND), a deficit hawk who at the time was chairman of the Senate Budget Committee, and Sen. Jeff Bingaman (D-NM), a low-key and experienced legislator with a moderate-to-liberal voting record. The Republican half of the Gang of Six was comprised of Senator Grassley (R-IA), the ranking Republican on the Senate Finance Committee and someone who had in the past worked with Baucus to produce bipartisan legislation, Sen. Mike Enzi (R-WY), a mild-mannered conservative who was the ranking Republican on the HELP Committee, and Sen. Olympia Snowe (R-ME),[21] a moder-

ate Republican whose support Senate Democrats—and
Baucus in particular—courted aggressively in the hopes
that they could claim the backing of at least one GOP
senator. The Gang of Six's talks continued throughout
the summer of 2009, as public support for health-care
reform continued to erode. In the end, it looked to
observers—particularly those who supported the reform effort—that Grassley had played Baucus for a
fool. The *Washington Post*'s Ezra Klein likened the Iowa
Republican to a manipulative boyfriend. He wrote:
"Grassley's friendship with Baucus is long and deep.
And he has made Baucus look like a weak, ineffectual
fool. He has absolutely hung him out to dry."[22]

Regardless of whether Baucus shared Klein's view
of his Republican colleague's behavior, he certainly
seemed to eventually come to the conclusion that
further negotiations were a fool's errand. He disbanded
the Gang of Six, and introduced his proposal on September 16, 2009. His bill expanded coverage to fewer
people than did the House bill, and did not include a
public option, which he saw as an insurmountable obstacle to garnering the 60 votes needed to overcome a
filibuster. The Finance Committee reported the bill by
a vote of 14–9 on October 13. Senator Snowe was the
only Republican on the Finance Committee to support
the bill.[23]

Senate Majority Leader Harry Reid introduced his
own bill that reconciled the differences between the

measures reported by the Finance and HELP commit-tees. His legislation did include a public option. As the Senate debated the measure for more than three weeks in December, Democrats worked furiously to maintain the support of Snowe, who by this time was seen as the only Republican senator still open to sup-porting the bill, as well as conservative Democratic senators. Sen. Ben Nelson (D-NE) was a key holdout and an opponent of the public option. Perhaps more surprisingly, Sen. Joseph Lieberman of Connecticut, a former Democrat who became an independent and who caucused with the Democrats for procedural pur-poses, made clear that he would vote with the Repub-licans to defeat the bill if it contained the public option.

Lieberman, who was the Democratic nominee for vice president as Al Gore's running mate in 2000, had undergone a political transformation since leaving the Democratic Party (which he did after losing the Demo-cratic primary to liberal challenger Ned Lamont in 2006). Although he had championed a proposal during his 2004 presidential campaign to let uninsured indi-viduals buy into Medicare (which some liberals saw as a viable alternative to the public option), he now indi-cated that such a provision would make the health-care bill unacceptable to him. Acquiescing to his and Nel-son's demands, the public option was removed from the underlying bill, and the effort to expand Medicare was abandoned.[24]

Most of what constituted the heart of the Democratic health-care reform effort, however, remained intact. It still created exchanges, provided subsides for people to purchase insurance, expanded Medicaid to cover more of the working poor, and imposed a host of new consumer protections for patients. Rather than impose a new tax on the wealthiest Americans (as the House bill had done), it instead proposed to tax the most expensive health plans, known as "Cadillac" plans. After a debate that monopolized Senate floor debate for much of the holiday season, Senate Democrats had rounded up the 60 votes necessary to break the Republicans' filibuster of the bill. Having voted finally to end debate on the measure on December 23, the Senate passed its health-care reform bill in a dramatic 60–39 vote on Christmas Eve. The bill passed with the support of all 60 Democrats. Snowe, the lone Republican to support the bill in the Finance Committee, joined with her party in the end to vote against it.[25]

IN SPECIAL ELECTION, MASSACHUSETTS GOES RED

Given the considerable differences between the House and Senate–passed health-care bills, negotiations between the two chambers to produce a reconciled package was sure to be an arduous process. Yet shortly after the New Year, the Democrats suffered a setback that no one had seen coming, and that was psychologically devastating to supporters of health reform. In a special election to fill the remainder of the late Sen. Ted Kennedy's (D-MA) term, the Democrats were caught flat-footed by a surprisingly strong challenge from Scott Brown, a state senator who opposed the health bill that had passed the Senate. The Democratic nominee, Martha Coakley, was also regarded as an exceptionally poor candidate. On January 19, Brown triumphed by a 52–47 percent margin, a result that reverberated around Capitol Hill instantly and powerfully, and seemed to have dealt a deathblow to health-care reform efforts.[26]

Stripped of their 60-vote supermajority, Democrats were now left without the votes they needed to defeat a Republican filibuster on the final health-care reform package that supporters hoped could be negotiated between the House and Senate. Moreover, the damage to the Democrats' psyche was not limited to those serving in the Senate. In the House, a number of stalwart supporters of the bill—including those who had fought for universal coverage for decades—seemed ready to give up. Rep. Barney Frank (D-MA), a long-time champion of liberal causes, released a statement that reflected Democrats' despair in the moment: "I feel strongly that the Democratic majority in congress must respect the process and make no effort to bypass the electoral results."[27] Rep. Bill Pascrell (D-NJ) urged a scaled-back effort to pass smaller health bills in a piecemeal fashion.[28]

What happened next was arguably one of the most remarkable political turnarounds in legislative history. On the night Scott Brown had prevailed in Massachusetts, President Obama met with Speaker Pelosi and Majority Leader Reid. The emerging consensus in Washington was indeed that health-care reform was dead. Yet there was still a way to pass a comprehensive reform bill, and it was fairly simple: the House could take up the Senate-passed bill. Once it cleared the House, Obama could sign it into law. Obama pressed Pelosi to do just that, but Pelosi countered that the Senate bill could not pass the House because it lacked sufficient support among their party's progressive wing.[29]

The compromise that began to take place was twofold. First, the House would pass the Senate bill. Then the Senate would take up a second bill implementing changes favored by House Democrats, and would do so under a special procedure called "budget reconciliation," which allows bills to be passed with a simple majority of 51 votes rather than the supermajority of 60. Senate Democratic leaders had been reluctant to employ this process because it was viewed as a bareknuckled tactic that might result in their losing the support of conservative Democrats. Having no other option at this point, however, Reid and his team began to re-consider their earlier stance.

★ OBAMA INTERVENES ★

President Obama, meanwhile, was no longer content to allow congressional leaders to remain in the driver's seat with respect to the centerpiece of his domestic agenda. Determined to rally support for health-care reform, he took a number of steps that would have been unthinkable just months earlier. First, on January 29—just ten days after Brown's victory—he attended a summit of House Republicans. Standing before the entire Republican conference, he made remarks supporting the legislation of which he had begun to take greater ownership. Then, in a move that attracted the kind of positive media coverage he had not enjoyed in quite some time, Obama began to take questions from his Republican adversaries. One by one, he took on his fiercest critics and pushed back against what he characterized as an intransigent and uncompromising opposition.[30] In the end, the event had gone just as Obama's team had hoped. His performance signaled to his allies that he was reenergized, and he seized the opportunity to build momentum behind passing the bill. In a televised summit a few weeks later, he tangled with Republican senators, including his former rival for the presidency, Sen. John McCain (R-AZ).[31]

With the effort to pass a health bill revived, Obama's team turned its attention to the House. Having given up any hope of Republican support, they worked in concert with Speaker Pelosi and her deputies to build a coalition of House Democrats that could pass the Senate bill. They lobbied moderate-to-conservative members of their party who were fighting for their political lives in their districts, as well as liberals who regarded the legislation as insufficiently progressive. When dealing with deficit hawks, the bill's supporters pointed to the bill's provisions to reduce the budget deficit. Other times, they appealed to members' consciences. Rep. Jason Altmire (D-PA), who represented a Republican-leaning district in Pennsylvania, received overtures from Obama as well as his chief of staff, former Rep. (and current Chicago mayor) Rahm Emanuel.[32] In the end, he would not budge.

A small voting block of vulnerable Democrats who opposed the House-passed bill in November, 2009, proved critical. Rep. John Boccieri, an Ohio Democrat facing intense headwinds as he fought for a second term in a Republican-leaning district, held an emotionally charged press conference to announce he was switching his vote. Invoking the story of an ill and uninsured constituent—whose name (Natoma Canfield) had become a rallying cry for Obama as he barnstormed the country in the final days of the battle for health reform—he said: "In this job, if I can save one life, one person, one Natoma, this job is worth it."[33] Rep. Bart Gordon, a Democrat who had represented a middle Tennessee district in the House for twenty-six years, also switched from "no" to "yes."[34]

The Democratic leadership also courted Rep. Betsy Markey, a freshman Democrat from Colorado who had toppled Rep. Marilyn Musgrave, Congress's leading antigay crusader, in 2008. Although she had defeated Musgrave by a surprising, ten-point margin, her district's Republican lean would make her reelection fight an uphill battle. On March 18, she announced she would vote in favor of the bill.[35] At the eleventh hour, on March 21, Rep. Brian Baird, who had represented a swing district in Southwest Washington State since 1998, also signaled he would vote "yes."[36] Rep. Suzanne Kosmas (D-FL), another freshman representative who had ridden the Democratic wave of 2008 to victory but who appeared vulnerable in 2010, had voted against the House bill back in November. This time, she voted with her party to pass the measure.[37]

One Democratic holdout was not a Blue Dog, but a longtime liberal voice in Democratic politics. Rep. Dennis Kucinich (D-OH) was a staunch supporter of a single-payer system, and had been adamant that he could not vote for a bill that further entrenched private insurers as a central component of the American health-care system. Obama, drawing on the personal relationship he had developed with Kucinich when they were both competing in the 2008 Democratic primary, made repeated personal appeals to the congressman from and one-time mayor of Cleveland. In the end, Kucinich voted "yes."[38]

★ FINAL PASSAGE ★

Increasingly confident that they had the votes needed to pass the bill, Democrats brought the measure to the House floor. As Speaker Pelosi gaveled the House into session at 1:00 p.m., she could be seen grinning as she made her way to the seat on the top tier of the dais at the front of the chamber. After the chaplain gave the prayer, she handed the Speaker's gavel to Rep. John Salazar (D-CO) to preside over the House.

Debate on the bill was at times tense and spirited, and both Speaker Pelosi and Minority Leader Boehner took the microphone to speak for their respective parties. Boehner, reflecting the predominant message of the Republican House conference that the Affordable Care Act (or what had come to be known as "Obamacare") was a cataclysmic mistake, was scathing in his criticism of the bill. Moreover, his conviction

that its passage cleared the way for his own Speakership was clearly evident:

> If we pass this bill, there will be no turning
> back. It will be the last straw for the American
> people. And in a democracy, you can only ignore
> the will of the people for so long and get away
> with it. And if we defy the will of our fellow cit-
> izens and pass this bill, we are going to be held to
> account by those who have placed us in their
> trust. We will have shattered those bonds of
> trust. I beg you. I beg each and every one of you
> on both sides of the aisle: do not further strike
> at the heart of this country and this institution
> with arrogance, for surely you will not strike with
> impunity. I ask each of you to vow never to let
> this happen again—this process, this defiance of
> our citizens. It is not too late to begin to restore
> the bonds of trust with our nation and return co-
> mity to this institution.[39]

Pelosi, who was about to go down in history as the
Speaker who presided over the passage of historic
health-care reform legislation long championed by her
party, was ebullient in her remarks:

> It would not be possible to talk about health
> care without acknowledging the great leadership

of Senator Edward Kennedy, who made health care his life's work. In a letter to President Obama before he passed away—he left the letter to be read after he died. Senator Kennedy wrote that: "Access to health care is the great unfinished business of our society." That is until today. . . . After a year of debate and hearing the calls of millions of Americans, we have come to this historic moment. Today, we have the opportunity to complete the great unfinished business of our society and pass health insurance reform for all Americans. That is a right and not a privilege.

In that same letter to the President, Senator Kennedy wrote, what is "at stake are not just the details of policy but . . . the character of our country." Americans will look back on this day as one which we honored the character of our country and honored our commitment to our nation's founders for a commitment to "life, liberty, and the pursuit of happiness."

As our colleague [Rep.] John Lewis [D-GA] has said, "We may not have chosen the time, but the time has chosen us." We have been given this opportunity. . . . I urge my colleagues in joining together in passing health insurance reform—making history, making progress, and restoring the American dream.[40]

At approximately 10:30 p.m., the House proceeded to vote on passage of the Senate's health-care reform bill. At 10:44, with the vote tally at 214–202 in favor of the bill, chants of "Four more votes!" could be heard from the Democratic side of the aisle. By 10:46 p.m., the tally was 217–207, with 7 members not yet having voted. As it became clear that the bill was going to pass—thereby clearing the way for Obama to sign it into law—Democratic members could be seen exchanging hugs and beginning to applaud. At 10:48, with all members having voted, the tally was 219–212. Representative Obey, in his role as the presiding officer, brought the vote to a close and announced the bill's passage.

Yet, health-care reform legislation was not yet passed in its entirety. Recall that House Democrats agreed to pass the Senate bill on the condition that both houses also vote on an additional "budget reconciliation" (see explanation above) bill containing a series of changes to the Senate bill favored by House Democrats—changes that, in the broader context of the Senate bill, were relatively minor. Thus, immediately following passage of the Senate's health-care bill, the House Democratic leadership brought up the second health-care measure.[41]

One late-breaking development that played out during floor consideration of the reconciliation bill concerned the issue of abortion. The Senate-passed bill that the House was to vote on shortly did not go as far as the original House measure in restricting federal funding for insurance plans that cover abortions. In order to bring Representative Stupak and his bloc of pro-life Democrats into the coalition to pass health-care reform, President Obama agreed to sign an executive order that effectively reiterated current law prohibiting public funding for abortions.

The debate over funding for abortion reached the House floor toward the end of floor debate on the reconciliation bill as Republicans used their motion to recommit—which was, as is customary, allowed by the rule—to try to insert antiabortion language into the bill's text. Republicans hoped that if pro-life Democrats voted with the GOP, the motion would pass, and leave Democratic leadership with a bill that was unacceptable to their caucus. As generally is the case (regardless of which party is in the minority), the motion to recommit was intended to torpedo the underlying health-care bill. In one of the more dramatic moments during floor debate on health-care reform, it was Stupak himself who rose to lead the opposition to the motion. Upon taking the microphone, Stupak was greeted by a round of applause from his Democratic colleagues seated behind him. In his remarks, he excoriated the Republican motion as cynical ruse:

> The motion to recommit purports to be a right-to-life motion, in the spirit of the Stupak

amendment. But as the author of the Stupak amendment, this motion is nothing more than an opportunity to continue to deny 32 million Americans health care. The motion is really a last-ditch effort of 98 years of denying Americans health care . . . Democrats guarantee all life from the unborn to the last breath of a senior citizen is honored and respected. For the unborn child, his or her mother will finally have pre- and postnatal care under our bill. If the child is born with mental problems, we provide medical care without bankrupting the family. For the Republicans to now claim that we send the bill back to committee [the technical purpose of a motion to recommit] under the guise of protecting life is disingenuous. This motion is really to politicize life, not prioritize life.[42]

In a sign of just how heated debate on this issue had become, Stupak was heckled by Republican members during his speech. Obey, who was still presiding over the House with the Speaker's gavel, warned members against such interruptions. Shortly thereafter, Rep. Randy Neugebauer (R-TX) shouted "Baby Killer!" at Stupak, drawing outraged protests from the Democratic side. Rep. Steny Hoyer (D-MD), then the Majority Leader, could be heard hushing his members, urging them to remain quiet.[43]

Ultimately, the House rejected the motion to recommit by a vote of 232–196.[44] The House then proceeded to pass the reconciliation bill by a vote of 220–211. The Senate then took up and passed the reconciliation bill four days later, on March 25. Yet in one last legislative wrinkle, Senate Republicans succeeded in removing two provisions from the House-passed reconciliation bill. (These provisions pertained to financial aid for college students, and were actually unrelated to health care.) Since the House and Senate had passed different versions of the reconciliation bill, the House then had to vote one last time to pass the measure as amended by the Senate, and did so later that day, by a vote of 220–207.[45] With that, legislative work on health-care reform was complete. President Obama signed both measures into law in Rose Garden ceremonies at the White House.

★ EPILOGUE ★

While Pelosi's Democratic caucus had succeeded in achieving arguably the greatest unfinished work of the New Deal and Great Society era, the ambitious effort to make such major change to social policy was not without political consequences. Just four years after having won back the majority, Democrats lost the House in a landslide defeat in the 2010 midterm elections. To be sure, a stubbornly sluggish economy also played a major role in laying the groundwork for the Republican wave. Yet it also seems clear that Democrats were, at least in the short term, punished by the voters for their efforts. Many vulnerable Democrats—and even those who were not considered to be vulnerable—went down to defeat. Representatives Betsy Markey (D-CO) and John Boccieri (D-OH), both of whom were referenced above, lost their reelection bids.

Rep. James Oberstar (D-MN), who had represented a sprawling district that included Minnesota's Iron Range, and who was not expected to face a difficult reelection fight, was also defeated. Yet Oberstar expressed a sentiment shared by other Democrats whose careers became causalities of the fight for universal health care: he had lost in service of what he had come to Congress to achieve, and he did not regret it. In a press conference after the election, he was asked whether he regretted his vote in favor of health-care reform. Oberstar, whose father was a founder of the Steelworkers' Union, recalled the history of those workers' fight for health insurance, and said: "I wish my father had lived to see the day that we cast that vote and we passed this legislation. . . ." He then went on to describe the bill's provisions, and the people whose suffering it had the power to alleviate. His voice growing uncharacteristically gravelly, he added: "I do not regret ever that vote. Ever."[46]

The customs of the House of Representatives can seem byzantine, its structure and procedures unnecessarily complex, and its culture mystifying. Livelier—and considerably less genteel—than the Senate, the House as an institution reflects the political reality of its composition. That is, it is the place where the micropolitical cultures of 435 localities converge, clash, and, in some form, coexist. Each member, to some degree, represents the political sensibilities and legacies of the district from which he or she was elected.

This stands in contrast to the "upper chamber," where senators represent entire, often politically diverse states. To be sure, the political culture of New York State differs in many ways from that of the State of Kansas. Yet the senators who represent New York do not exclusively represent New York City and its surrounding areas. They represent Chautauqua County, which borders western Pennsylvania. Similarly, while Kansas's two senators represent its more conservative rural and suburban areas, they also represent the city of Topeka, as well as Lawrence, a liberal bastion. In other words, senators represent states in their entirety, including their cities, college towns, rural areas, and suburbs. House members, however, are anchored to smaller and often more politically homogenous constituencies.

The chamber's rules put the majority party firmly in control of its legislative agenda. After a first two years in which President Obama saw much of his domestic policy platform enacted, he now largely uses his limited executive authority to pursue his agenda. Since the Democrats did not regain control of the House in the 2014 midterm elections, the legislative standoff may well continue through the end of Obama's presidency, with the president using his executive powers to make policy changes, and with the Republican-controlled House effectively pursuing a shadow governing agenda. The House could serve as a legislative engine for substantive change once again if the Democrats regain control of the chamber in 2016 while electing a Democratic president—or if the Republicans win the White House while retaining their majority. For now, the status quo seems likely to endure, with Speaker Boehner serving as the president's most prominent adversary in Washington, yet constantly looking over his right shoulder to monitor a fractious conference of House Republicans with a conservative wing eager for greater confrontation.

It is my hope that this book will provide readers with a guide by which to observe and better understand the House as it plays a critical role in national debates. I intend for it to serve as a tool by which readers can better follow the national debates that shape government policy and ultimately affect all of our lives.

☆ NOTES ☆

INTRODUCTION

1. www.nytimes.com/2013/01/04/us/politics/Boehner-liked
   -but-not-feared-keeps-a-job.html?ref=politics

2. www.nytimes.com/2013/01/04/us/politics/new-congress
   -begins-with-wishes-of-comity-but-battles-ahead.html
   ?pagewanted=all

3. www.politico.com/news/stories/0111/47831.html

4. www.nytimes.com/2013/01/05/business/after-fiscal-deal
   -tax-code-may-be-most-progressive-since-1979.html?ref
   =bushtaxcuts

5. www.cnn.com/election/2012/results/race/house

I. ELECTION TO THE U.S. HOUSE

1. www.thefiscaltimes.com/Articles/2013/07/10/The-Outra
geous-Costs-of-Being-Elected-to-Congress.aspx#
page1

2. minnesota.publicradio.org/collections/special/2004
/campaign/results/data/html/cd/cd_1data.html

3. www.mprnews.org/story/2006/11/08/1dist

4. hamptonroads.com/2010/11/rigell-reclaims-us-house-seat
-gop-win-over-nye

5. www.nj.com/news/index.ssf/2010/11/winner_congress_nj
_3rd_distric.html

6. elections.nytimes.com/2010/results/illinois

7. www.nytimes.com/1996/10/24/us/illinois-lawmaker
-proves-a-tough-target-for-gop.html?pagewanted=1

8. www.fec.gov/pubrec/fe1996/hril.htm

9. articles.chicagotribune.com/2012-11-07/news/chi-duck
worth-walsh-election-results-illinois-8th-district-2012
1106_1_kaitlin-fahey-duckworth-campaign-manager
-democrat-tammy-duckworth

10. www.nytimes.com/2008/11/29/us/politics/29web
-duckworth.html?fta=y

11. www.foxnews.com/politics/2009/02/03/obama-nomina
tes-duckworth-veterans-affairs-post/

12. bioguide.congress.gov/scripts/biodisplay.pl?index
=R000580

13. roskam.house.gov/media-center/blog-posts/peter-roskam
-consummate-conservative-warrior

14. www.nytimes.com/cq/2007/01/17/cq_2132.html?page
wanted=print

15. www.nytimes.com/2010/01/22/us/politics/22scotus
.html

16. www.nytimes.com/2010/03/27/us/politics/27campaign
.html

2. THE LEADERSHIP

1. www.washingtonpost.com/politics/a-house-gop-leadership
-primer-what-do-the-speaker-majority-leader-and-whip
-actually-do/2014/06/16/3abdcb80-f57c-11e3-a3a5-42be
35962a52_story.html

2. www.nytimes.com/2013/01/04/us/politics/new-congress
-begins-with-wishes-of-comity-but-battles-ahead.html
?pagewanted=all

3. www.politico.com/news/stories/1107/6757.html

4. www.newrepublic.com/article/politics/84568/kilgore-ging
   rich-liberal-policies

5. www.huffingtonpost.com/2012/02/26/newt-gingrich
   -moderate_n_1302205.html

6. www.newrepublic.com/article/politics/84568/kilgore
   -gingrich-liberal-policies

7. www.nytimes.com/2011/12/21/us/politics/the-long-run
   -conservatives-remain-suspicious-of-gingrich.html?page
   wanted=all

8. www.c-span.org/video/?171083-1/speaker-orders-cameras
   -pan-chamber

9. www.mcclatchydc.com/2012/08/20/162796/analysis-how
   -the-death-of-compromise.html

10. thehill.com/homenews/house/88201-pelosi-achieves
    -biggest-political-victory-of-her-career

11. content.time.com/time/nation/article/0,8599,1558504,00
    .html

12. www.nytimes.com/2003/11/23/us/final-push-congress
    -overview-sharply-split-house-passes-broad-medicare
    -overhaul.html?src=pm&pagewanted=2.
        www.forbes.com/2009/11/19/republican-budget
    -hypocrisy-health-care-opinions-columnists-bruce-bartlett
    .html

13. www.washingtonpost.com/wp-dyn/articles/A63387
    -2004Sep30.html

14. www.politico.com/news/stories/1110/45672.html

15. www.democraticwhip.gov/content/hoyer-announces
    -whip-team-113th-congress

16. www.washingtonpost.com/wp-srv/politics/special/clinton
    /stories/livingston122098.htm

17. www.cnn.com/ALLPOLITICS/stories/1998/11/18/gop
    .leadership/

18. www.washingtonpost.com/wp-dyn/content/article/2006
    /01/16/AR2006011600997.html

19. www.politico.com/news/stories/1110/45077.html

20. www.foxnews.com/story/2007/11/27/former-house-speaker
    -dennis-hastert-submits-official-resignation-letter-to/

21. www.washingtonpost.com/wp-dyn/content/article/2006
    /02/02/AR2006020201046.html

22. abcnews.go.com/Politics/john-boehner-speaker-republi-
    cans-pledge-cut-grow-majority/story?id=12541614

23. thehill.com/blogs/ballot-box/senate-races/127213-long
    time-house-gop-leader-blunt-wins-senate-seat-

24. www.foxnews.com/politics/2012/11/07/gop-holds-house
    -dems-hold-senate/

25. www.nytimes.com/2013/10/19/us/politics/thomas-foley
    -former-house-speaker-dies-at-84.html?pagewanted=all
    &_r=0

26. www.politico.com/story/2014/06/2014-virginia-primary
    -big-money-eric-cantor-107699.html?hp=f1.
        www.nbcnews.com/politics/elections/eric-cantor-blew
    -168k-steak-houses-brat-spent-122k-overall-n128126

27. www.washingtonpost.com/blogs/the-fix/wp/2014/06/10
    /david-brat-just-beat-eric-cantor-who-is-he/

28. articles.baltimoresun.com/1991-04-20/news/1991110026
    _1_mo-udall-humor-carter

29. www.nytimes.com/1981/07/30/politics/30REAG.html

30. www.usnews.com/news/articles/2004/06/21/ronald
    -reagan-tip-oneill-and-the-clash-of-the-titans

31. www.nytimes.com/1981/07/30/politics/30REAG.html

3. THE RULES COMMITTEE

1. www.washingtonpost.com/wp-dyn/content/article/2010
   /03/15/AR2010031503742.html?hpid=topnews

2. www.politico.com/news/stories/0310/34508.html

3. online.wsj.com/news/articles/SB10001424052748703909
   8045751235127730700080talkingpointsmemo.com/dc
   /gop-plans-to-implement-the-demon-pass-they-once
   -decried

4. www.washingtonpost.com/opinions/dana-milbank-republi
   cans-gagging-hypocrisy/2014/06/09/c279db60-f016-11e3
   -914c-1fbd0614e2d4_story.html

5. www.rollcall.com/news/-36008-1.html

6. www.politico.com/magazine/story/2014/01/the-most
   -closed-congress-in-history-101794.html

4. STANDING COMMITTEES

1. edworkforce.house.gov/committee/committeehistory
   .htm

2. www.washingtonpost.com/wp-dyn/content/article/2007
   /01/05/AR2007010501877.html?referrer=emailarticle

3. www.politico.com/news/stories/1108/15822.html

4. itk.thehill.com/homenews/campaign/81-leach-exit-would
   -give-dems-opening

5. latimesblogs.latimes.com/culturemonster/2009/06/obama
   -humanities-appointment.html

6. www.salon.com/2011/02/08/harman_pelosi_congress/

7. www.washingtonpost.com/wp-dyn/content/article/2006/12/01/AR2006120100496.html

8. Obey, David. "The Chairmanship," in *Raising Hell for Justice: The Washington Battles of a Heartland Progressive*. Madison, WI: University of Wisconsin, 2007

9. thehill.com/policy/international/205034-house-panel-subpoenas-kerry-to-testify-on-new-benghazi-emails

5. LEGISLATIVE SERVICE ORGANIZATIONS

1. www.cbcfinc.org/2013-archive/653-congressional-black-caucus-foundation-hosts-ceremonial-swearing-in-for-cbc-members.html

2. thehill.com/special-reports/congressional-black-caucus-september-2013/323187-congressional-black-caucus-history-

3. www.nytimes.com/2008/08/10/magazine/10politics-t.html?pagewanted=all

4. abcnews.go.com/blogs/politics/2010/12/tim-scott-will-not-join-congressional-black-caucus-my-campaign-was-never-about-race/

5. thegrio.com/2013/11/22/black-senators-diverge-on-joining-congressional-black-caucus/

6. prospect.org/article/let-steve-cohen-join-cbc

7. www.washingtonpost.com/wp-dyn/content/article/2010 /07/19/AR2010071905006.html

8. history.house.gov/Exhibitions-and-Publications/HAIC /Historical-Essays/Strength-Numbers/Caucus-Conference/

9. chc-hinojosa.house.gov/membership

10. www.politico.com/news/stories/0211/49017.html

11. library.cqpress.com/cqalmanac/document.php?id=cqal95 -1099473

12. library.cqpress.com/cqalmanac/document.php?id=cqal95 -1099473.
    www.washingtonpost.com/wp-dyn/content/arti cle/2010/11/02/AR2010110205483.html

13. Herzog, Arthur. "The Candidate," in *McCarthy for President: The Candidacy That Toppled a President, Pulled a New Generation into Politics, and Moved the Country Toward Peace.* New York: Writers Club, 2003, p. 52.

14. testaae.greenwood.com/doc_print.aspx?fileID=MDX &chapterID=MDX-1563&path=books/greenwood

15. query.nytimes.com/mem/archive/pdf?res=9B0DE4D711 3CE13ABC4A52DFB766838A679EDE

16. query.nytimes.com/mem/archive/pdf?res=9B0DE4D711 3CE13ABC4A52DFB766838A679EDE

17. www.nytimes.com/2011/05/27/opinion/27Perlstein.html ?pagewanted=all

18. www.washingtonpost.com/wp-srv/politics/daily/dec98 /udall14.htm

19. Obey, David. "Digging In for the Long Haul," in *Raising Hell for Justice: The Washington Battles of a Heartland Progressive*. Madison, WI: University of Wisconsin, 2007, pp. 134–35.

20. www.washingtonpost.com/national/thomas-s-foley -former-house-speaker-dies-at-84/2013/10/18/7d2c7df4-380d -11e3-ae46-e4248e75c8ea_story.html

21. www.nytimes.com/1989/07/24/obituaries/frank-thomp son-70-career-in-congress-ended-with-abscam.html

22. Obey, David. "Two New Jobs, One Secret War," in *Raising Hell for Justice: The Washington Battles of a Heartland Progressive*. Madison, WI: University of Wisconsin, 2007, p. 235.

23. www.nytimes.com/2001/11/16/us/ex-rep-bob-eckhardt -88-liberal-democrat-of-texas.html

24. clerk.house.gov/member_info/electioninfo/1980election.pdf

25. clerk.house.gov/member_info/electioninfo/1980election.pdf

26. clerk.house.gov/member_info/electioninfo/1980election.pdf

27. Obey, David. "The Chairmanship." in *Raising Hell for Justice: The Washington Battles of a Heartland Progressive.* Madison, WI: University of Wisconsin, 2007, pp. 292–297

28. www2.mnhs.org/library/findaids/00462.xmlwww.defense.gov/bios/biographydetail.aspx?biographyid=310

6. FLOOR DEBATE

1. www.gpo.gov/fdsys/pkg/BILLS-113hr4801eh/pdf/BILLS-113hr4801eh.pdf

2. nymag.com/daily/intelligencer/2010/02/anthony_weiner_the_republican.html

3. www.c-span.org/video/?55475-1/house-session'

4. www.youtube.com/watch?v=eKYMOtODQT4

5. capitolwords.org/date/2006/05/17/H2691-7_providing-for-further-consideration-of-h-con-res-3/

6. www.brookings.edu/research/testimony/2010/04/22-filibuster-binder

7. CASE STUDY—THE AFFORDABLE CARE ACT

1. www.washingtontimes.com/news/2008/oct/24/kennedy-secretly-crafts-health-care-plan/?page=all

2. www.washingtonpost.com/wp-dyn/content/article/2008
   /11/11/AR2008111102511.html

3. www.aallnet.org/main-menu/publications/llj/llj-archives
   /vol-105/no-2/2013-7.pdf

4. www.aallnet.org/main-menu/publications/llj/llj-archives
   /vol-105/no-2/2013-7.pdf

5. politicalticker.blogs.cnn.com/2009/07/24/talks-break-down
   -intra-party-tension-heats-up-for-house-democrats/

6. politicalticker.blogs.cnn.com/2009/07/24/talks-break-down
   -intra-party-tension-heats-up-for-house-democrats/

7. www.cnn.com/2009/POLITICS/07/10/house.health.care/

8. www.nytimes.com/2009/07/30/us/politics/30health.html?
   _r=1&

9. www.nytimes.com/2009/07/30/us/politics/30health.html?
   _r=1&

10. www.huffingtonpost.com/2009/08/06/tampa-town-hall
    -on-health_n_253478.html

11. www.nytimes.com/2009/08/08/us/politics/08townhall.html

12. www.cbsnews.com/news/calif-rep-says-he-wont-waste
    -urine-on-mans-leg/

13. www.cnn.com/2009/POLITICS/09/24/kennedy
.replacement/

14. politicalticker.blogs.cnn.com/2009/09/02/cnn-poll-keep
-working-on-health-care-reform/

15. iowaindependent.com/18456/grassley-government
-shouldnt-decide-when-to-pull-the-plug-on-grandma

16. www.nytimes.com/2009/09/10/us/politics/10obama.html
?pagewanted=all

17. thecaucus.blogs.nytimes.com/2009/09/15/blogging-the
-house-action-on-wilson/?module=ArrowsNav&con
tentCollection=Politics&action=keypress&region=Fixed
Left&pgtype=Blogs

18. www.aallnet.org/main-menu/publications/llj/llj-archives
/vol-105/no-2/2013-7.pdf

19. politics.nytimes.com/congress/votes/111/house/1/884

20. www.nytimes.com/2009/11/08/health/policy/08health
.html?pagewanted=all

21. www.newrepublic.com/article/75077/how-they-did-it

22. voices.washingtonpost.com/ezra-klein/2009/09/chuck
_grassleys_legislative_te.html

23. www.politico.com/news/stories/1009/28235.html

24. www.boston.com/news/health/articles/2009/12/16
/public_option_out_democrats_press_on/

25. www.nytimes.com/2009/12/25/health/policy/25health.html

26. www.nytimes.com/2010/01/20/us/politics/20election
.html?_r=0

27. www.politico.com/livepulse/0110/Frank_Congress_should
_not_bypass_the_election_results.html

28. thehill.com/homenews/house/77459-house-dems
-warming-to-scaled-back-healthcare-reform

29. www.washingtonpost.com/wp-dyn/content/article/2010
/03/22/AR2010032203729_3.html?sid=ST20100
32304326

30. abcnews.go.com/blogs/politics/2010/01/into-the-ryans-den
-president-obama-attends-house-gop-caucus-for-lively
-give-and-take/

31. www.cbsnews.com/news/obama-to-mccain-the-elections
-over/

32. abcnews.go.com/WN/HealthCare/health-care-endg
ame-president-obama-dems-duel-deadline/story?id=100
75048

33. www.youtube.com/watch?v=KCBaN2kmfHk

34. votesmart.org/candidate/27071/bart-gordon?categoryId =38#.U9prRoBdVAU

35. blogs.denverpost.com/thespot/2010/03/18/markey-will -vote-health-reform-bill/

36. seattletimes.com/html/politicsnorthwest/2011403571_br ianbairdtoswitchtoyesvoteonhealthreform.html

37. votesmart.org/public-statement/493913/kosmas-helps -pass-fiscally-responsible-health-care-reform-legislation# .U9pmaoBdVAU

38. talkingpointsmemo.com/dc/kucinich-to-vote-yes-on -health-care-reform-here-s-why

39. congress.gov/crec-2010-03-21-house-bk2.pdf

40. congress.gov/crec-2010-03-21-house-bk2.pdf

41. abcnews.go.com/Politics/HealthCare/health-care-bill -back-house-vote-republican-challenges/story?id=1020 5547

42. congress.gov/crec-2010-03-21-house-bk2.pdf

43. www.youtube.com/watch?v=PFWYWzjGzOU. www.cbsnews.com/videos/stupak-called-baby-killer/

★ NOTES ★

44. voices.washingtonpost.com/44/2010/03/house-defeats
    -gop-motion-to-re.html

45. abcnews.go.com/Politics/HealthCare/health-care-bill
    -back-house-vote-republican-challenges/story?id=1020
    5547

46. www.youtube.com/watch?v=oTEHQN_d1uA

APPENDIX A: SPEAKERS OF THE UNITED STATES HOUSE OF REPRESENTATIVES

NAME	STATE	YEARS SERVED	DATE ELECTED SPEAKER
Frederick Augustus Conrad Muhlenberg	PA	1789–1791	Apr. 1, 1789
Jonathan Trumbull Jr.	CT	1791–1793	Oct. 24, 1791
Frederick Augustus Conrad Muhlenberg	PA	1793–1795	Dec. 2, 1793
Jonathan Dayton	NJ	1795–1799	Dec. 7, 1795
Theodore Sedgwick	MA	1799–1801	Dec. 2, 1799
Nathaniel Macon	NC	1801–1807	Dec. 7, 1801
Joseph Bradley Varnum	MA	1807–1811	Oct. 26, 1807

NAME	STATE	YEARS SERVED	DATE ELECTED SPEAKER
Henry Clay	KY	1811–1813	Nov. 4, 1811
Langdon Cheves	SC	1814–1815	Jan. 19, 1814
Henry Clay	KY	1815–1820	Dec. 4, 1815
John W. Taylor	NY	1820–1821	Nov. 15, 1820
Philip Pendleton Barbour	VA	1821–1823	Dec. 4, 1821
Henry Clay	KY	1823–1825	Dec. 1, 1823
John W. Taylor	NY	1825–1827	Dec. 5, 1825
Andrew Stevenson	VA	1827–1834	Dec. 3, 1827
John Bell	TN	1833–1835	Jun. 2, 1834
James Knox Polk	TN	1835–1839	Dec. 7, 1835
Robert Mercer Taliaferro Hunter	VA	1839–1841	Dec. 16, 1839
John White	KY	1841–1843	May 31, 1841
John Winston Jones	VA	1843–1845	Dec. 4, 1843
John Wesley David	IN	1845–1847	Dec. 1, 1845
Robert Charles Winthrop	MA	1847–1849	Dec. 6, 1847
Howell Cobb	GA	1849–1851	Dec. 22, 1849
Boyd, Linn	KY	1851–1855	Dec. 1, 1851
Nathaniel Prentice Banks	MA	1855–1857	Feb. 2, 1856
James Lawrence Orr	SC	1857–1859	Dec. 7, 1857
William Pennington	NJ	1859–1861	Feb. 1, 1860
Galusha Aaron Grow	PA	1861–1863	Jul. 4, 1861
Schuyler Colfax	IN	1863–1869	Dec. 7, 1863

NAME	STATE	YEARS SERVED	DATE ELECTED SPEAKER
Theodore Medad Pomeroy	NY	1869	Mar. 3, 1869
James Gillespie Blaine	ME	1869–1875	Mar. 4, 1869
Michael Crawford Kerr	IN	1875–1877	Dec 6, 1875
Samuel Jackson Randall	PA	1875–1881	Dec. 4, 1876
Joseph Warren Keifer	OH	1881–1883	Dec. 5, 1881
John Griffin Carlisle	KY	1883–1889	Dec. 3, 1883
Thomas Brackett Reed	ME	1889–1891	Dec. 2, 1889
Charles Frederick Crisp	GA	1891–1895	Dec. 8, 1891
Thomas Brackett Reed	ME	1895–1899	Dec. 2, 1895
David Bremner Henderson	IA	1899–1901	Dec. 4, 1899
David Bremner Henderson	IA	1901–1903	Dec. 2, 1901
Joseph Gurney Cannon	IL	1903–1911	Nov. 9, 1903
James Beauchamp "Champ" Clark	MO	1911–1919	Apr. 4, 1911
Frederick Huntington Gillett	MA	1919–1925	May 19, 1919
Nicholas Longworth	OH	1925–1931	Dec. 7, 1925
John Nance Garner	TX	1931–1933	Dec. 7, 1931

NAME	STATE	YEARS SERVED	DATE ELECTED SPEAKER
Henry Thomas Rainey	IL	1933–1935	Mar. 9, 1933
Joseph Wellington Byrns	TN	1935–1936	Jan. 3, 1935
William Brockman Bankhead	AL	1936–1940	Jun. 4, 1936
Samuel Taliaferro Rayburn	TX	1939–1947	Sep. 16, 1940
Joseph William Martin Jr.	MA	1947–1949	Jan. 3, 1947
Samuel Taliaferro Rayburn	TX	1949–1953	Jan. 3, 1949
Joseph William Martin Jr.	MA	1953–1955	Jan. 3, 1953
Samuel Taliaferro Rayburn	TX	1955–1962	Jan.5, 1955
John William McCormack	MA	1962–1971	Jan. 10, 1962
Carl Bert Albert	OK	1971–1977	Jan. 21, 1971
Thomas "Tip" Philip O'Neill Jr.	MA	1977–1987	Jan. 4, 1977
James Claude Wright Jr.	TX	1987–1989	Jan. 6, 1987
Thomas Stephen Foley	WA	1989–1995	Jun. 6, 1989
Newton Leroy Gingrich	GA	1995–1999	Jan. 4, 1995
John Dennis Hastert	IL	1999–2007	Jan. 6, 1999
Nancy Pelosi	CA	2007–2011	Jan. 4, 2007
John Andrew Boehner	OH	2011–2015	Jan. 5, 2011

HOUSE COMMITTEE ON AGRICULTURE

Subcommittee on Department Operations, Oversight, and Nutrition

Subcommittee on Conservation, Energy, and Forestry

Subcommittee on General Farm Commodities and Risk Management

Subcommittee on Livestock, Rural Development, and Credit

Subcommittee on Horticulture, Research, Biotechnology, and Foreign Agriculture

HOUSE COMMITTEE ON APPROPRIATIONS

Subcommittee on Agriculture, Rural Development, Food and Drug Administration, and Related Agencies

Subcommittee on Commerce, Justice, Science, and Related
   Agencies
Subcommittee on Defense
Subcommittee on Energy and Water Development, and Related
   Agencies
Subcommittee on Financial Services and General Government
Subcommittee on Homeland Security
Subcommittee on Interior and Environment, and Related
   Agencies
Subcommittee on Labor, Health and Human Services, Educa-
   tion, and Related Agencies
Subcommittee on Legislative Branch
Subcommittee on Military Construction, Veterans Affairs, and
   Related Agencies
Subcommittee on State, Foreign Operations, and Related
   Programs
Subcommittee on Transportation, Housing and Urban Devel-
   opment, and Related Agencies

HOUSE COMMITTEE ON ARMED SERVICES

Subcommittee on Intelligence, EmergingThreats and Capa-
   bilities
Subcommittee on Oversight and Investigations
Subcommittee on Military Personnel
Subcommittee on Readiness
Subcommittee on Seapower and Projection Forces

Subcommittee on Strategic Forces
Subcommittee on Tactical Air and Land Forces

HOUSE COMMITTEE ON BUDGET

[No Subcommittees]

HOUSE COMMITTEE ON EDUCATION AND THE WORKFORCE

Subcommittee on Early Childhood, Elementary, and Secondary Education
Subcommittee on Health, Employment, Labor, and Pensions
Subcommittee on Higher Education and Workforce Training
Subcommittee on Workforce Protections

HOUSE COMMITTEE ON ENERGY AND COMMERCE

Subcommittee on Commerce, Manufacturing, and Trade
Subcommittee on Communications and Technology
Subcommittee on Energy and Power
Subcommittee on Environment and Economy
Subcommittee on Health
Subcommittee on Oversight and Investigations

HOUSE COMMITTEE ON ETHICS

[No Subcommittees]

HOUSE COMMITTEE ON FOREIGN AFFAIRS

Subcommittee on Africa, Global Health, Global Human Rights, and International Organizations

Subcommittee on Asia and the Pacific

Subcommittee on Europe, Eurasia, and Emerging Threats

Subcommittee on the Middle East and North Africa

Subcommittee on Terrorism, Nonproliferation, and Trade

Subcommittee on the Western Hemisphere

HOUSE COMMITTEE ON FINANCIAL SERVICES

Subcommittee on Capital Markets and Government Sponsored Enterprises

Subcommittee on Financial Institutions and Consumer Credit

Subcommittee on Housing and Insurance

Subcommittee on Monetary Policy and Trade

Subcommittee on Oversight and Investigations

HOUSE COMMITTEE ON HOMELAND SECURITY

Subcommittee on Border and Maritime Security

Subcommittee on Cybersecurity, Infrastructure Protection, and Security Technologies

Subcommittee on Counterterrorism and Intelligence

Subcommittee on Emergency Preparedness, Response, and Communications

Subcommittee on Oversight and Management Efficiency
Subcommittee on Transportation Security

HOUSE COMMITTEE ON HOUSE ADMINISTRATION

[No Subcommittees]

HOUSE PERMANENT SELECT COMMITTEE ON INTELLIGENCE

Subcommittee on Oversight
Subcommittee on Terrorism, HUMINT, Analysis, and Counter-
intelligence
Subcommittee on Technical and Tactical Intelligence

HOUSE COMMITTEE ON THE JUDICIARY

Subcommittee on the Constitution and Civil Justice
Subcommittee on Courts, Intellectual Property, and the Inter-
net
Subcommittee on Crime, Terrorism, Homeland Security, and
Investigations
Subcommittee on Immigration and Border Security
Subcommittee on Regulatory Reform, Commercial, and Anti-
trust Law

HOUSE COMMITTEE ON NATURAL RESOURCES

Subcommittee on Energy and Mineral Resources

Subcommittee on Fisheries, Wildlife, Oceans, and Insular Affairs

Subcommittee on Indian and Alaska Native Affairs

Subcommittee on Public Lands and Environmental Regulation

Subcommittee on Water and Power

HOUSE COMMITTEE ON OVERSIGHT AND GOVERNMENT REFORM

Subcommittee on Economic Growth, Job Creation, and Regulatory Affairs

Subcommittee on Energy Policy, Health Care, and Entitlements

Subcommittee on Federal Workforce, U.S. Postal Service, and the Census

Subcommittee on Government Operations

Subcommittee on National Security

HOUSE COMMITTEE ON RULES

Subcommittee on the Legislative and Budget Process

Subcommittee on Rules and Organization of the House

HOUSE COMMITTEE ON SCIENCE, SPACE, AND TECHNOLOGY

Subcommittee on Energy

Subcommittee on Environment

Subcommittee on Oversight

Subcommittee on Research and Technology
Subcommittee on Space

HOUSE COMMITTEE ON SMALL BUSINESS

Subcommittee on Agriculture, Energy, and Trade
Subcommittee on Contracting and the Workforce
Subcommittee on Economic Growth, Tax and Capital Access
Subcommittee on Health and Technology
Subcommittee on Investigations, Oversight, and Regulations

HOUSE COMMITTEE ON TRANSPORTATION AND INFRASTRUCTURE

Subcommittee on Aviation
Subcommittee on Coast Guard and Maritime Transportation
Subcommittee on Economic Development, Public Buildings,
    and Emergency Management
Subcommittee on Highways and Transit
Subcommittee on Railroads, Pipelines, and Hazardous Materials
Subcommittee on Water Resources and Environment

HOUSE COMMITTEE ON VETERANS' AFFAIRS

Subcommittee on Disability Assistance and Memorial Affairs
Subcommittee on Economic Opportunity
Subcommittee on Health
Subcommittee on Oversight and Investigations

HOUSE COMMITTEE ON WAYS AND MEANS

Subcommittee on Health

Subcommittee on Human Resources

Subcommittee on Oversight

Subcommittee on Select Revenue Measures

Subcommittee on Social Security

Subcommittee on Trade

☆ INDEX ☆

Armed Services Committee, 70,
160–61
Armey, Dick, 38
Army Corps of Engineers, 72
Assistant Democratic Leader,
40
authorizing committee, 68
automobile industry, 62

"backbencher," 38
Baird, Brian, 128
banking scandal, 85
Baucus, Max, 109–10, 113,
120–21
Bayh, Birch, 86
Biggert, Judy, 15
bills
appropriations, 56
debate under suspension of
rules, 49, 91
report of, 59, 66, 68
rules accompanying, 49, 92
signed into law, 58
standing committees and,
58–59
votes on, 22, 24, 32, 33–35,
46–49, 52–55, 93
Bingaman, Jeff, 120
Blue Dogs Coalition, 79–80,
107, 113–15
Blunt, Roy, 41, 44
Boccieri, John, 127, 136
Boehner, John
Affordable Care Act and, 47,
129–30
ally of, 52
Obama and, 2, 46–47, 138
as Speaker of the House, 1–2,
23, 41–42, 44

Boggs, Hale, 45, 84
Booker, Cory, 77
Borger, Gloria, 46
Bradley, Jeb, 16
Brat, Dave, 44
Brown, Scott, 53, 124–25
budget
deficit reduction, 127
reconciliation, 53–55, 125,
132–33, 135
resolution, 71, 98–104
Budget Committee, 71, 161
Burr, Aaron, 104
Bush, George W.
policy of, 33–34, 55, 65
as unpopular, 11
Bush-era tax cuts, 3–4

campaign committees,
16–18
Canfield, Natoma, 127–28
Cantor, Eric, 43–44
Carter, Jimmy, 86
Castor, Kathy, 116
caucuses
CBC, 76–78
Conference/Caucus
Chairman, 22
Congressional Hispanic
Caucus, 78–79
definition of, 76
Democratic Caucus, 24
CBC. *See* Congressional Black
Caucus
chairmen
Conference/Caucus
Chairman, 22
Rules Committee, House,
51–52

of standing committees,
59–61, 60–61, 63–66,
91–92
term limits for, 60
Church, Frank, 86
*Citizens United v. Federal
Election Commission*, 19
civil rights legislation, 81–82, 89
Clay, William Lacy, Jr., 78
Clay, William Lacy, Sr., 78
Clinton, Bill, 37, 79, 109, 111
Clinton, Hillary, 95
closed rules, 49–50, 57
Clyburn, James, 39–40
CNN poll, 117
Coakley, Martha, 124
coalitions, 76
Blue Dogs, 79–80, 107,
113–15
Cohen, Steve, 77–78
Colmer, William, 83
Commerce, Manufacturing, and
Trade subcommittee, 66
Commission on Legislative
Review, 88
Committee of the Whole, 92
Committee on Economic and
Educational Opportunities,
60
committees. *See also* standing
committees
authorizing, 68
campaign, 16–18
DCCC, 16–17
Finance Committee, Senate,
120
health-care reform and,
111–18
HELP, 109, 120, 122

NRCC, 16–17
Rules and Administration
Committee, Senate, 50
tax-writing, 68
Conference/Caucus Chairman,
22
Congressional Black Caucus
(CBC), 76–78
Congressional Hispanic
Caucus, 78–79
Congressional Quarterly, 89
Congressional Record, 30
Congressman, 8
Congressman-Elect, 20–21
Congresswoman, 8
Congresswoman-Elect, 20–21
Conrad, Kent, 120
Conservative Opportunity
Society, 28
Constitution, U.S., 7, 23
Craig, Jim, 16–17
C-Span, 29, 35

DCCC. *See* Democratic
Congressional Campaign
Committee
Deal, Nathan, 80
death panels, 118
debates
on amendments, 49–50,
55–57, 92–95
floor, 50, 55, 90–105
on health insurance, 93
over appropriations bills, 56
Rules Committee, House,
and, 48–57, 92
under suspension of rules,
49, 91
Deem and Pass, 54

DeLauro, Rosa, 66
DeLay, Tom, 15, 32, 35, 38,
  40–41
DeMint, Jim, 77
Democratic Caucus, 24
Democratic Congressional
  Campaign Committee
  (DCCC), 16–17
Democratic Study Group
  (DSG), 80–89
Demon Pass, 54
Department of Defense, 70
Department of Transportation,
  72
Department of Veterans Affairs,
  72
deputy whips, 22, 36–38
Dingell, John D., 61–63
Dornan, Bob, 94
DSG. See Democratic Study
  Group
Duckworth, Tammy, 14

Eckhardt, Bob, 86
economic stimulus, 2, 4
Education and Labor
  Committee, 59–61, 67
Education and the Workforce
  Committee, 61, 67, 91, 161
Edwards, John, 95
elections, 7–21
  advertising and, 10, 18–19
  campaign committees, 16–18
  cycle, 3
  527s in, 18
  fundraising and costs of,
    9–10, 18–19, 43–44
  to leadership, 44–45
  political outsiders in, 10–14

Senate, 7
special, 20, 123–26
transition period, 20–21
vacant seats, 8, 20
voter turnout and, 20
wave election, 4
Emanuel, Rahm, 127
Employment Non-
  Discrimination Act
  (ENDA), 94–96
Energy and Commerce
  Committee, 58, 59, 61, 63,
  67–68, 113–15
  subcommittees, 66, 161
Energy and Power
  subcommittee, 66
Energy Department, 70
environmental issues, 62–64
Enzi, Mike, 120
Ethics Committee, 35, 73, 161
"everyman," 10
executive powers, 138

farm subsidies, 58, 69
federal spending
  Budget Committee and, 71
  increases, 4
  social programs and, 3, 56
filibuster, 53, 105, 123, 124
Finance Committee, Senate, 120
financial regulatory laws, 2, 4
Financial Services Committee,
  70–71, 162
527s, 18
floor debate, 50, 55, 90–105
  definition of, 90
  previous question motion
    during, 104–5
  in Senate, 97